TestSMART®

for Reading Skills and Comprehension—Grade 7

Aligned to State and National Standards

Help for

Basic Reading Skills

State Competency Tests

Achievement Tests

by

Lori Mammen

Printed in the United States of America.

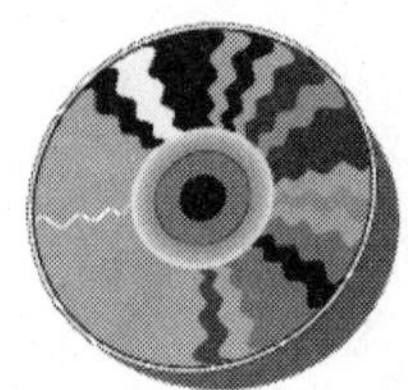

Book Cover: Kirstin Simpson **Book Design:** Educational Media Services

ISBN 1–57022–202–9

Contents

Welcome to *TestSMART*®!!

It's just the tool you need
to help students review important reading skills and
prepare for standardized reading tests!

Introduction

During the past several years, an increasing number of American students have faced some form of state-mandated competency testing in reading. While several states use established achievement tests, such as the Iowa Test of Basic Skills (ITBS), to assess students' reading ability, other states' reading assessments focus on the skills and knowledge emphasized in their particular reading curriculum. Texas, for example, has administered a state-developed assessment since 1980. The New York State Testing Program began in 1999 and tests both fourth- and eighth-grade students in reading.

Whatever the testing route, one point is very clear: the trend toward more and more competency testing is widespread and intense. By the spring of 1999, 48 states had adopted some type of reading assessment for students at various grade levels. In some states, these tests are "high-stakes" events that determine whether a student is promoted to the next grade level in school.

The emphasis on competency tests has grown directly from the national push for higher educational standards and accountability. Under increasing pressure from political leaders, business people, and the general public, policy-makers have turned to testing as a primary way to easure and improve student performance.

Although experienced educators know that such test results can reveal only a small part of a much broader educational picture, state-mandated competency tests have gained a strong foothold. Teachers must find effective ways to help their students prepare for these tests—and this is where *TestSMART*® plays an important role.

What's inside this book?

Designed to help students review and practice important reading and test-taking skills, *TestSMART*® includes reproducible practice exercises in the following areas—

- vocabulary
- comprehension
- study skills

In addition, each *TestSMART*® book includes—

- a master skills list based on reading standards of several states
- a comprehensive vocabulary list
- complete answer keys for multiple-choice questions
- scoring guidelines and rubrics for open-ended questions
- a reproducible answer sheet

The content of each section of *TestSMART* ® is outlined below.

Vocabulary: This section of *TestSMART* ® includes 19 practice exercises with questions that focus on—

- demonstrating knowledge of root words and structural cues (Practices 1–4)
- using context clues to determine word meaning (Practices 5-9)
- recognizing the correct meaning of a word with multiple meanings (Practices 10-12)
- demonstrating knowledge of synonyms and antonyms (Practices 13–16)
- demonstrating knowledge of word analogies (Practices 17–19)

(Note: Vocabulary skills addressed in this section are also addressed in the reading comprehension section of TestSMART ®.)

Comprehension: This section of *TestSMART* ® includes—

- 12 reading passages, which include nonfiction, fiction, and poetry selections
- multiple-choice and open-ended questions for each passage
- tag-lines that identify the skill(s) addressed in each question

Reading skills addressed in this section include—

- determining the meaning of words *(root words, context clues, multiple-meaning words, synonyms/antonyms)*
- identifying supporting ideas *(facts/details, sequential order, written directions, setting)*
- summarizing written texts *(main idea, summary of major ideas/themes/ procedures)*
- perceiving relationships and recognizing outcomes *(cause/effect, predictions, similarities/differences)*
- analyzing information to make inferences and generalizations *(inferences, interpretations/ conclusions, generalizations, character analysis)*
- recognizing points of view, propaganda, and statements of fact/opinion *(fact/opinion, author's purpose)*
- reading, analyzing, and interpreting literature *(genre identification, genre characteristics, literary elements, figurative language)*

Study Skills: This section of *TestSMART* ® includes 14 practice exercises that focus on identifying and using sources of different types of information (graphic sources, parts of a book, dictionary skills). Specific skills addressed in this section include—

- using parts of a book (Practice 1)
- interpreting charts, diagrams, and graphs (Practices 2-4, 11-12)
- using a library card catalog (Practice 5)
- interpreting practical reading material (Practices 6-7)
- recognizing and using dictionary skills (Practice 8)
- identifying appropriate sources of information (Practice 9-10)
- interpreting maps (Practices 13-14)

Master Skills List/Correlation Chart: The reading skills addressed in *TestSMART®* are based on the reading standards and/or test specifications from several different states. No two states have identical wordings for their skills lists, but there are strong similarities from one state's list to another. Of course, the skills needed for effective reading do not change from one place to another. The Master Skills List for Reading (page 9) represents a synthesis of the reading skills emphasized in various states. Teachers who use this book will recognize the skills that are stressed, even though the wording of a few objectives may vary slightly from that found in their own state's test specifications. The Master Skills Correlation Chart (page 10) offers a place to identify the skills common to both *TestSMART®* and a specific state competency test.

Vocabulary List: A list of vocabulary words appears on page 126. This list includes many of the words tested in the vocabulary section of this book and in questions that accompany some of the passages. Teachers and students can use this list to create—

- word games
- word walls
- writing activities
- "word-of-the-day" activities
- synonym/antonym charts
- word webs
- analogies
- … and more

A word of caution: In general, teachers should not ask students to memorize the words and their meanings. While some tests ask students to simply "know" the meaning of selected vocabulary words, the majority of tests emphasize using structural cues and context clues to determine the meaning of unfamiliar words encountered during reading.

Answer Keys: Complete answer keys for multiple-choice questions appear on pages 118-120.

Scoring Guidelines and Rubrics: The scoring guidelines and sample rubrics on pages 121-125 provide important information for evaluating responses to open-ended questions. (*Note: If a state's assessment does not include open-ended questions, teachers may use the open-ended items in TestSMART® as appropriate for their students.*) The scoring guidelines indicate the expected contents of successful responses. For example, if an open-ended question asks students to create a new title for a passage and give reasons for their answer, the scoring guideline for that question suggests specific points that students should include in the answer.

The sample rubrics allow teachers to rate the overall effectiveness and thoroughness of an answer. Once again, consider the example of creating a new title for a passage and supporting the answer with specific reasons. The corresponding rubric for that question indicates the number and quality of the reasons necessary to earn a score of "4" (for an effective, complete response) or a score of "1" (for an ineffective, incomplete response).

How to Use This Book

Effective Test Preparation: What is the most effective way to prepare students for any reading competency test? Experienced educators know that the best test preparation includes three critical components—

- a strong curriculum that includes the content and skills to be tested
- effective and varied instructional methods that allow students to learn content and skills in many different ways
- targeted practice that familiarizes students with the specific content and format of the test they will take

Obviously, a strong curriculum and effective, varied instructional methods provide the foundation for all appropriate test preparation. Contrary to what some might believe, merely "teaching the test" performs a great disservice to students. Students must acquire knowledge, practice skills, and have specific educational experiences which can never be included on tests limited by time and in scope. For this reason, books like *TestSMART* ® should **never** become the heart of the curriculum or a replacement for strong instructional methods.

Targeted Practice: *TestSMART* ® does, however, address the final element of effective test preparation (targeted test practice) in the following ways—

- *TestSMART* ® familiarizes students with the content usually included in competency tests.
- *TestSMART* ® familiarizes students with the general format of such tests.

When students become familiar with both the content and the format of a test, they know what to expect on the actual test. This, in turn, improves their chances for success.

Using *TestSMART* ®: Used as part of the regular curriculum, *TestSMART* ® allows teachers to—

- pretest skills needed for the actual test students will take
- determine students' areas of strength and/or weakness
- provide meaningful test-taking practice for students
- ease students' test anxiety
- communicate test expectations and content to parents

Other Suggestions for Instruction: *TestSMART* ® can serve as a springboard for other effective instructional activities that help with test preparation.

Group Work: Teacher and students work through selected practice exercises together, noting the kinds of questions and the range of answer choices. They discuss common errors for each kind of question and strategies for avoiding these errors.

Predicting Answers: Students predict the correct answer before reading the given answer choices. This encourages students to think through the question rather than focus on finding the right answer. Students then read the given answer choices and determine which one, if any, matches the answer they have given.

Developing Test Questions: Once students become familiar with the format of test questions, they develop "test-type" questions for other assigned reading (e.g., science, social studies).

Vocabulary Development: Teacher and students foster vocabulary development in all subject areas through the use of word walls, word webs, word games, synonym/antonym charts, analogies, word categories, "word-of-the-day" activities, etc.

Two-Sentence Recaps: Students regularly summarize what they have read in one or two sentences. For fiction, students use the basic elements (setting, characters, problem, solution) to guide their summaries. For nonfiction, students use the journalist's questions (who, what, where, when, why) for the same purpose. The teacher may also list 3–5 key words from a reading selection and direct students to write a one- to two-sentence summary that includes the given words.

Generalizations: After students read a selection, the teacher states a generalization based on the reading, and students provide specific facts and details to support the generalization; or the teacher provides specifics from the selection, and students state the generalization.

Master Skills List

I. Determine the meaning of words in written texts

A. Use root words and other structural cues to recognize new words
B. Use context clues to determine word meaning
C. Recognize correct meaning of words with multiple meanings
D. Demonstrate knowledge of synonyms, antonyms, and homophones
E. Choose the correct word to complete an analogy

II. Identify supporting ideas

A. Identify relevant facts and details
B. Use text structure (e.g., headings, subheadings) to locate relevant facts and details
C. Sequence events in chronological order (e.g., story events, steps in process)
D. Follow written directions

III. Summarize a variety of written texts

A. Determine the main idea or essential message of a text
B. Paraphrase or summarize the major ideas, themes, or procedures of a text

IV. Perceive relationships and recognize outcomes

A. Identify cause and effect relationships in a text
B. Make and verify predictions with information from a text
C. Connect, compare, and contrast ideas, themes, and issues across texts
D. Respond to texts by making observations/connections, speculating, questioning, etc.

V. Analyze information in order to make inferences and generalizations

A. Make and explain inferences (e.g., main idea, conclusion, moral, cause/effect)
B. Support interpretations/conclusions with information from text(s)
C. Make generalizations based on information from a text

VI. Recognize points of view, propaganda, and statements of fact and opinion

A. Distinguish fact from opinion in a text
B. Identify the author's purpose
C. Recognize logical, ethical, and emotional appeals
D. Analyze positions, arguments, and evidence presented by an author
E. Identify bias and propaganda

VII. Read, analyze, and interpret literature

A. Identify genres of fiction, nonfiction, and poetry
B. Identify characteristics representative of a given genre
C. Identify important literary elements (e.g., theme, setting, plot, character, conflict)
D. Recognize/interpret figurative language (e.g., simile, metaphor, hyperbole, idiom, allusion)
E. Recognize use of sound devices (e.g., rhyme, alliteration, onomatopoeia)

VIII. Identify and use sources of different types of information

A. Use and interpret graphic sources of information (e.g., charts, graphs)
B. Use reference resources and the parts of a book (e.g., index) to locate information
C. Recognize and use dictionary skills

Master Skills Correlation Chart

Use this chart to identify the skills included on a specific state competency test. To correlate the skills to a specific state's objectives, find and mark those skills common to both. The first column shows a sample correlation based on the Texas Assessment of Knowledge and Skills (TAKS).

		Sample Correlation ↓	
I.	**Determine the meaning of words in written texts**		
	A. Use root words and other structural cues to recognize new words	*	
	B. Use context clues to determine word meaning	*	
	C. Recognize correct meaning of words with multiple meanings	*	
	D. Demonstrate knowledge of synonyms, antonyms, and homophones		
	E. Choose the correct word to complete an analogy		
II.	**Identify supporting ideas**		
	A. Identify relevant facts and details	*	
	B. Use text structure (e.g., headings, subheadings) to locate relevant facts and details	*	
	C. Sequence events in chronological order	*	
	D. Follow written directions		
III.	**Summarize a variety of written texts**		
	A. Determine the main idea or essential message of a text	*	
	B. Summarize the major ideas, themes, or procedures of a text	*	
IV.	**Perceive relationships and recognize outcomes**		
	A. Identify cause and effect relationships	*	
	B. Make and verify predictions with information from text	*	
	C. Connect, compare, and contrast ideas, themes, and issues across texts	*	
	D. Respond to texts by making observations/connections, speculating, questioning		
V.	**Analyze information in order to make inferences and generalizations**		
	A. Make and explain inferences	*	
	B. Support interpretations/conclusions with information from a text	*	
	C. Make generalizations based on information from a text	*	
VI.	**Recognize points of view, propaganda, and statements of fact and opinion**		
	A. Distinguish fact from opinion	*	
	B. Identify the author's purpose	*	
	C. Recognize logical, ethical, and emotional appeals		
	D. Analyze positions, arguments, and evidence presented by an author	*	
	E. Identify bias and propaganda	*	
VII.	**Read, analyze, and interpret literature**		
	A. Identify genres of fiction, nonfiction, and poetry		
	B. Identify characteristics representative of a given genre		
	C. Identify important literary elements	*	
	D. Recognize/interpret figurative language		
	E. Recognize use of sound devices		
VIII.	**Identify and use sources of different types of information**		
	A. Use and interpret graphic sources of information	*	
	B. Use reference resources and the parts of a book to locate information		
	C. Recognize and use dictionary skills		

Vocabulary

I. Determine the meaning of words in written texts

A. Use root words and other structural cues to recognize new words
B. Use context clues to determine word meaning
C. Recognize correct meaning of words with multiple meanings
D. Demonstrate knowledge of synonyms and antonyms
E. Choose the correct word to complete an analogy

Practice 1: Root Words and Structural Cues

Directions: Read each question. On your answer sheet, darken the circle for each correct response.

1. Which word probably comes from the Latin word *absurdus*, which means "stupid"?

A absent

B abstain

C absurd

D astound

2. The word **insulate** probably comes from the Latin word—

A *insultare*, meaning to spring or leap

B *instruere*, meaning to build

C *instare*, meaning to stand

D *insula*, meaning island

3. Which word probably comes from the Latin word *constringere*, meaning "to press together"?

A stretch

B strange

C constrict

D consent

4. In the words **irresponsible** and **irregular**, the prefix **ir** means—

A with

B not

C after

D again

5. In the words **autobiography** and **autograph**, the prefix **auto** means—

A again

B sign

C book

D self

6. The word **migrate** comes from the Latin word *migrare*, meaning "to move." Which word is most closely related in meaning to the word **migrate**?

A mileage

B mighty

C immigrant

D miracle

7. Which word probably comes from the Latin word *fidelis*, meaning "faithful"?

A future

B fidelity

C fluid

D final

8. In the words **navigator** and **supervisor**, the suffix **or** means—

A one who does

B against

C to move

D self

I.A Use root words and other structural cues to recognize new words

Practice 2: Root Words and Structural Cues

Directions: Read each question. On your answer sheet, darken the circle for each correct response.

1. Which word probably comes from the Latin word *exsistere*, which means "to come into being"?

   A exact

   B execute

   C explode

   D existence

2. Which word probably comes from the Greek word *dynamikos*, which means "powerful"?

   A dented

   B dynamic

   C distance

   D directing

3. Which word probably comes from the Greek word *eidolon*, meaning "image"?

   A longitude

   B dollar

   C ideal

   D idol

4. In the words **disagreeable** and **distrustful**, the prefix **dis** means—

   A for

   B again

   C not

   D with

5. The word **consumer** probably comes from the Latin word—

   A *consultare*, meaning to consider

   B *consumere*, meaning to take-up

   C *corrigere*, meaning to lead straight

   D *consentire*, meaning to feel

6. Which word probably comes from the Latin word *ignorare*, meaning "not to know"?

   A iguana

   B ignite

   C ignorance

   D unnatural

7. In the words **interactive** and **interchange**, the prefix **inter** means—

   A above

   B between

   C around

   D from

8. In the words **suitable** and **honorable**, the suffix **able** means—

   A having or owning

   B belonging to

   C full of

   D capable of being

I.A Use root words and other structural cues to recognize new words

Practice 3: Root Words and Structural Cues

Directions: Read each question. On your answer sheet, darken the circle for each correct response.

1. Which word probably comes from the Latin word *sapor*, which means "to taste"?

A satisfy

B support

C savage

D savor

2. Which word probably comes from the Latin word *rus*, which means "country"?

A rush

B rural

C rust

D runt

3. Which word probably comes from the Greek word *polein,* meaning "to sell"?

A mopping

B monster

C monopoly

D pollen

4. In the words **mishandle** and **misfit**, the prefix **mis** means—

A before

B back

C wrong

D for

5. The word **simulate** probably comes from the Latin word—

A *multus*, meaning many

B *sincerus*, meaning real

C *simplicitas*, meaning simple

D *similis*, meaning like

6. Which word probably comes from the Latin word *polis*, meaning "city"?

A polite

B political

C polish

D pole

7. In the words **semicircle** and **semifinal**, the prefix **semi** means—

A twice

B before

C around

D half

8. In the words **manhood** and **falsehood**, the suffix **hood** means—

A condition or quality

B position

C action

D person

I.A Use root words and other structural cues to recognize new words

Practice 4: Root Words and Structural Cues

Directions: Read each question. On your answer sheet, darken the circle for each correct response.

1. Which word probably comes from the Middle English word *astonen*, which means "to amaze"?

   A astray
   B astound
   C assure
   D assault

2. Which word probably comes from the Greek word *nautes*, which means "sailor"?

   A natural
   B native
   C astonish
   D astronaut

3. Which word probably comes from the Latin word *vicus,* meaning "neighborhood"?

   A vital
   B violate
   C victorious
   D vicinity

4. In the words **imprison** and **import**, the prefix **im** means—

   A over
   B within
   C around
   D away

5. The word **astronomy** probably comes from the Greek word—

   A *astron*, meaning star
   B *asthenes*, meaning weak
   C *noton*, meaning back
   D *monos*, meaning alone

6. Which word probably comes from the Greek word *pathos*, meaning "emotions"?

   A pattern
   B thought
   C attitude
   D sympathy

7. In the words **ingratitude** and **incredible**, the prefix **in** means—

   A under
   B without
   C completely
   D superior

8. In the words **foreseen** and **forerunner**, the prefix **fore** means—

   A behind
   B under
   C within
   D in front

I.A Use root words and other structural cues to recognize new words

Practice 5: Context Clues

Directions: Read the following sentences. Then choose the best word to fit in the blank. On your answer sheet, darken the circle for the correct answer.

1. Martha slept away from the other children because her cold was ____________ .

A concealed
B contagious
C comforting
D constant

2. Please ____________ my name on the bracelet.

A enlist
B produce
C consult
D engrave

3. I didn't know who wrote the letter because the handwriting was not ____________ .

A judicial
B complete
C legible
D fluent

4. The auto accident was a ____________ event for the Martinez family.

A reliable
B worthy
C tragic
D sympathetic

5. The school dance will not succeed without enough ____________ .

A repetition
B potential
C publicity
D suggestion

6. Students who misbehave will be ____________ from the dance.

A ejected
B existed
C deceived
D relieved

7. With her singing ability, Rebecca is ____________ to become a star.

A illustrated
B performed
C confided
D destined

8. Tony likes to dress in ____________ clothing.

A apparent
B predictable
C fashionable
D effective

I.B Use context clues to determine word meaning

Practice 6: Context Clues

Directions: Read the following sentences. Then choose the best word to fit in the blank. On your answer sheet, darken the circle for the correct answer.

1. After their argument, you could feel the ___________ between them.

A enchantment
B tension
C criticism
D intention

2. They will ___________ the old building before building a new one.

A depart
B design
C defect
D demolish

3. Serious problems sometimes call for ____________ solutions.

A drastic
B enthusiastic
C flawed
D illustrated

4. Who will be the guest speaker at the ____________ of the new school?

A consideration
B institution
C dedication
D complication

5. ______________ flowers can sometimes look as nice as real ones.

A general
B displayed
C artificial
D approved

6. If you go shopping in the mall, expect to be ______________ in the huge crowds.

A limited
B jostled
C expelled
D astounded

7. Before the test, make a ___________ review of your class work.

A thorough
B splendid
C suggested
D visual

8. Icy roads cause ________________ driving conditions.

A invisible
B resistant
C reliable
D treacherous

I.B Use context clues to determine word meaning

Practice 7: Context Clues

Directions: Read the following sentences. Then choose the best word to fit in the blank. On your answer sheet, darken the circle for the correct answer.

1. Have you been ______________ for measles and whooping cough?
   - **A** standardized
   - **B** affected
   - **C** vaccinated
   - **D** tolerated

2. How often do you ______________ with your pen pal in China?
   - **A** perceive
   - **B** function
   - **C** respond
   - **D** correspond

3. To gain ___________ to the event, Jose needed a stamped ticket.
   - **A** entry
   - **B** reversal
   - **C** intent
   - **D** keepsake

4. The school's strict uniform policy does not allow for any _____________ in dress.
   - **A** simplicity
   - **B** effectiveness
   - **C** authority
   - **D** variation

5. Sunita asked for special _____________ because she had been ill.
   - **A** dedication
   - **B** consideration
   - **C** intention
   - **D** conscience

6. Only _____________ employees can expect a raise at the end of the year.
   - **A** restless
   - **B** voluntary
   - **C** reliable
   - **D** standard

7. Her writing is entertaining because she always includes _________ details.
   - **A** urgent
   - **B** vivid
   - **C** complicated
   - **D** predictable

8. Marco does not want the car if it has a serious ____________ .
   - **A** position
   - **B** dispute
   - **C** defect
   - **D** barrier

I.B Use context clues to determine word meaning

Practice 8: Context Clues

Directions: Read the following sentences. Then choose the best word to fit in the blank. On your answer sheet, darken the circle for the correct answer.

1. A _______________ witness appears honest and believable.
   A public
   B vital
   C critical
   D credible

2. The accident caused injury to her _____________ organs.
   A dependent
   B internal
   C visual
   D mobile

3. As part of the _____________ section, Tanya plays the kettledrum.
   A enthusiastic
   B recital
   C percussion
   D persuasive

4. I cannot force you to participate because membership is ______________ .
   A profitable
   B creative
   C voluntary
   D independent

5. Jay enjoys hugs from his _____________ baby sister.
   A affectionate
   B agreeable
   C enchanting
   D sentimental

6. Mrs. George could not hire the young man because he did not have the proper ____________________ .
   A preferences
   B qualifications
   C coincidences
   D institutions

7. The sitter tried to ____________ the baby girl when her parents left for the party.
   A distinct
   B dispute
   C distrust
   D distract

8. Marianna saved a napkin and rosebud as ____________ from the dance.
   A bulletins
   B idols
   C keepsakes
   D fascinations

I.B Use context clues to determine word meaning

Practice 9: Context Clues

Directions: Read the following sentences. Then choose the best word to fit in the blank. On your answer sheet, darken the circle for the correct answer.

1. Without water and sunlight, the plants will not _____________ .

   A recycle

   B display

   C thrive

   D acquire

2. In the fairy tale, the king _________ the wicked troll from the kingdom.

   A expelled

   B criticized

   C clinched

   D resisted

3. The firefighter received an award for her _____________ actions during the flood.

   A restless

   B fatal

   C fascinating

   D heroic

4. Soon after the robbery, the police were in ____________ of the criminals.

   A revolt

   B succession

   C pursuit

   D distrust

5. After the accident, the principal wanted to _____________ new safety rules.

   A inspire

   B install

   C institute

   D intend

6. The young boy had no ____________ record, so the judge did not send him to jail.

   A constant

   B previous

   C external

   D internal

7. The excited crowd cheered as the ________________ team circled the field.

   A predictable

   B dynamic

   C complimentary

   D victorious

8. The chef made sure the kitchen was kept clean and _______________ .

   A sufficient

   B sanitary

   C considerate

   D fundamental

I.B Use context clues to determine word meaning

Practice 10: Multiple-Meaning Words

Directions: Read each numbered sentence. Then choose the correct meaning for the bolded word as it is used in the sentence. On your answer sheet, darken the circle for the correct word.

1. Do not **dwell** on unimportant problems.

A live

B haunt

C focus

D speak

2. When will you **apply** for college?

A request admission

B use

C put on

D put into action

3. She **fractured** her arm in two places.

A abused

B faulted

C disrupted

D broke

4. He conducts his life according to high **ideals**.

A perfections

B objects of honor

C patterns

D standards

5. After the flood, normal school activities were **suspended** for several days.

A hung

B dismissed

C delayed

D supported

6. Selling cigarettes to **minors** is illegal.

A lesser sizes

B underaged persons

C areas of study

D scales

7. Such unusual movies usually don't appeal to the **masses**.

A religious ceremonies

B bodies of matter

C common people

D measurements

8. The television game show failed because it did not have enough **sponsors**.

A responsible people

B advertisers

C legislators

D godparents

I.C Recognize correct meaning of words with multiple meanings

Practice 11: Multiple-Meaning Words

Directions: Read each numbered sentence. Then choose the correct meaning for the bolded word as it is used in the sentence. On your answer sheet, darken the circle for the correct word.

1. Parents can **discipline** their children in many gentle ways.

A study and learn
B correct and control
C obey and follow
D lecture and hear

2. If you arrive late for the meeting, show **consideration** to those who are already seated.

A careful thought
B treatment
C payment
D courtesy

3. My father's business **associate** attended the party.

A college degree
B friend
C member
D partner

4. **Brooding** over our problems will not solve them.

A protecting
B sitting
C worrying
D covering

5. To exit the computer program, **depress** the escape key.

A lower
B sadden
C push down
D weaken

6. That bank is an old and respected **institution** in our community.

A custom
B hospital
C building
D organization

7. Long ago, a man usually took great pleasure in **courting** the girl he loved.

A behaving
B pursuing
C inviting
D marrying

8. During the ceremony, my mother was **elevated** to the position of vice president.

A promoted
B increased
C lifted
D elated

I.C Recognize correct meaning of words with multiple meanings

Practice 12: Multiple-Meaning Words

Directions: Read each numbered sentence. Then choose the correct meaning for the bolded word as it is used in the sentence. On your answer sheet, darken the circle for the correct word.

1. If you ever have a problem, you can **bank** on Ross to help you.

   A operate
   B tilt
   C depend
   D save

2. The doctor said I should not experience any **acute** pain after the surgery.

   A accurate
   B sharp
   C rapid
   D shrill

3. Strangers needed a pass to visit the school **compound**.

   A combination
   B complication
   C chemical substance
   D campus

4. I used my **canceled** check to prove when I bought my stereo.

   A removed
   B ceased
   C erased
   D marked

5. The actress wore a blue blouse with a lace **fringe**.

   A benefit
   B view
   C border
   D group

6. We will **dedicate** the beginning of the meeting to new business.

   A write
   B set aside
   C open
   D bless

7. Its unusual for Marco to **display** his feelings so openly.

   A hold up
   B exhibit
   C express
   D spread out

8. The **atmosphere** in the locker room was uncomfortable after the team lost the championship.

   A air
   B mood
   C pressure
   D suggestion

I.C Recognize correct meaning of words with multiple meanings

Practice 13: Synonyms and Antonyms

Directions: For numbers 1-5, find the word that has the same or about the same meaning as the bolded word. On your answer sheet, darken the circle for the correct word.

1. **abundant** food at the party
   - **A** scarce
   - **B** tasty
   - **C** prepared
   - **D** plentiful

2. **acquire** the proper forms
   - **A** obtain
   - **B** lose
   - **C** request
   - **D** file

3. a wide **boulevard**
   - **A** necktie
   - **B** field
   - **C** avenue
   - **D** building

4. **brandish** a sword
   - **A** shatter
   - **B** conceal
   - **C** wave
   - **D** remove

5. **fatal** accident
   - **A** avoidable
   - **B** dangerous
   - **C** minor
   - **D** deadly

Directions: For numbers 6-10, find the word that has the opposite meaning of the bolded word. On your answer sheet, darken the circle for the correct word.

6. a **garbled** message
   - **A** confused
   - **B** clear
   - **C** repeated
   - **D** simple

7. **dynamic** performance
   - **A** strong
   - **B** incredible
   - **C** weak
   - **D** repeated

8. **criticize** a decision
   - **A** disapprove
   - **B** ignore
   - **C** examine
   - **D** praise

9. **fashionable** clothing
   - **A** stylish
   - **B** tattered
   - **C** dated
   - **D** expensive

10. **external** appearance
    - **A** obvious
    - **B** unnecessary
    - **C** final
    - **D** inner

I.D Demonstrate knowledge of synonyms, antonyms, and homophones

Practice 14: Synonyms and Antonyms

Directions: For numbers 1-5, find the word that has the same or about the same meaning as the bolded word. On your answer sheet, darken the circle for the correct word.

1. a complete **falsehood**
   - A truth
   - B lie
   - C statement
   - D reality

2. **restless** sleep
   - A relaxed
   - B deep
   - C lengthy
   - D disturbed

3. **potential** problems
   - A actual
   - B serious
   - C possible
   - D simple

4. a black **shroud**
   - A decision
   - B mark
   - C veil
   - D cloudiness

5. **minimal** pay
   - A regular
   - B overtime
   - C increased
   - D least

Directions: For numbers 6-10, find the word that has the opposite meaning of the bolded word. On your answer sheet, darken the circle for the correct word.

6. **sufficient** funds
   - A inadequate
   - B available
   - C acceptable
   - D hidden

7. **urgent** request
   - A complicated
   - B necessary
   - C answered
   - D unimportant

8. **unreliable** employee
   - A changeable
   - B trustworthy
   - C temporary
   - D permanent

9. **radiant** light
   - A brilliant
   - B flickering
   - C dim
   - D colorful

10. **condemned** prisoner
    - A reformed
    - B punished
    - C regretful
    - D released

I.D Demonstrate knowledge of synonyms, antonyms, and homophones

Practice 15: Synonyms and Antonyms

Directions: For numbers 1-5, find the word that has the same or about the same meaning as the bolded word. On your answer sheet, darken the circle for the correct word.

1. **ardent** fan
   - **A** disinterested
   - **B** regular
   - **C** carefree
   - **D** enthusiastic

2. **covet** someone's wealth
   - **A** ignore
   - **B** receive
   - **C** require
   - **D** desire

3. a strong **competitor**
   - **A** teammate
   - **B** athlete
   - **C** rival
   - **D** coach

4. the necessary **implements**
   - **A** methods
   - **B** tools
   - **C** plans
   - **D** locations

5. **implore** sincerely
   - **A** plead
   - **B** respond
   - **C** react
   - **D** prefer

Directions: For numbers 6-10, find the word that has the opposite meaning of the bolded word. On your answer sheet, darken the circle for the correct word.

6. **scenic** view
   - **A** breathtaking
   - **B** unsightly
   - **C** changing
   - **D** distant

7. **perceptive** answers
   - **A** intelligent
   - **B** wise
   - **C** dense
   - **D** repeated

8. **convenient** location
   - **A** handy
   - **B** central
   - **C** popular
   - **D** distant

9. **distinct** features
   - **A** obvious
   - **B** attractive
   - **C** vague
   - **D** unique

10. **economical** use of supplies
    - **A** thrifty
    - **B** cheap
    - **C** wasteful
    - **D** daily

I.D Demonstrate knowledge of synonyms, antonyms, and homophones

Practice 16: Synonyms and Antonyms

Directions: For numbers 1-5, find the word that has the same or about the same meaning as the bolded word. On your answer sheet, darken the circle for the correct word.

1. **fascinating** speaker
   - A dull
   - B professional
   - C charming
   - D unprepared

2. **filthy** clothing
   - A soiled
   - B fresh
   - C laundered
   - D simple

3. the actor's **flawed** performance
   - A ideal
   - B opening
   - C rehearsed
   - D imperfect

4. endless **repetition**
   - A procedure
   - B criticism
   - C duplication
   - D advice

5. **violate** the rules
   - A respect
   - B alter
   - C disobey
   - D dissolve

Directions: For numbers 6-10, find the word that has the opposite meaning of the bolded word. On your answer sheet, darken the circle for the correct word.

6. **stingy** neighbor
   - A nearest
   - B generous
   - C tight
   - D hostile

7. showing **malice** toward none
   - A spite
   - B honesty
   - C resentment
   - D compassion

8. **exact** answers
   - A careless
   - B accurate
   - C provided
   - D missing

9. **constrict** the throat
   - A soothe
   - B tighten
   - C expand
   - D cure

10. **elated** students
    - A joyous
    - B countless
    - C exhausted
    - D miserable

I.D Demonstrate knowledge of synonyms, antonyms, and homophones

Practice 17: Analogies

Directions: Read each analogy. Find the word that correctly completes each analogy. On your answer sheet, darken the circle for the correct word.

1. **Rocks** are to **geologists** as **stars** are to _______________ .

   A navigators
   B scientists
   C astronomers
   D instructors

2. **End** is to **begin** as **cease** is to _______________ .

   A activate
   B repeat
   C renew
   D regard

3. **Frown** is to **unpleasant** as **smile** is to _______________ .

   A feature
   B unfortunate
   C forgiving
   D agreeable

4. **Office** is to **work** as **playground** is to _______________ .

   A park
   B vacation
   C participation
   D amusement

5. **One** is to **two** as **monologue** is to _______________ .

   A script
   B dialogue
   C performance
   D skit

6. **School** is to **student** as **neighborhood** is to _______________ .

   A visitor
   B governor
   C resident
   D property

7. **Body** is to **soul** as **physical** is to _______________.

   A actual
   B spiritual
   C visual
   D potential

8. **Loser** is to **defeated** as **winner** is to _______________ .

   A unqualified
   B satisfactory
   C maximum
   D victorious

I.E Choose the correct word to complete an analogy

Practice 18: Analogies

Directions: Read each analogy. Find the word that correctly completes each analogy. On your answer sheet, darken the circle for the correct word.

1. **Candy** is to **wrapper** as **fruit** is to ___________ .
   - **A** seed
   - **B** rind
   - **C** leaf
   - **D** plant

2. **Company** is to **president** as **church** is to ___________ .
   - **A** worshipper
   - **B** conductor
   - **C** parson
   - **D** prayer

3. **Prisoners** are to **riot** as **sailors** are to ___________ .
   - **A** voyage
   - **B** navigation
   - **C** mutiny
   - **D** defeat

4. **Forests** are to **damp** as **deserts** are to ___________ .
   - **A** sandy
   - **B** bright
   - **C** arid
   - **D** distant

5. **Happiness** is to **joy** as **anger** is to ___________ .
   - **A** upset
   - **B** wrath
   - **C** spite
   - **D** dread

6. **Advertisement** is to **jingle** as **campaign** is to ___________ .
   - **A** slogan
   - **B** saying
   - **C** candidate
   - **D** voting

7. **Porcupine** is to **prickly** as **tiger** is to ___________ .
   - **A** dangerous
   - **B** fierce
   - **C** striped
   - **D** sleek

8. **Car** is to **steer** as **ship** is to ___________ .
   - **A** handle
   - **B** captain
   - **C** navigate
   - **D** drive

I.E Choose the correct word to complete an analogy

Practice 19: Analogies

Directions: Read each analogy. Find the word that correctly completes each analogy. On your answer sheet, darken the circle for the correct word.

1. **Work** is to **salary** as **retire** is to ________ .

   A payment
   B restfulness
   C vacation
   D pension

2. **Idea** is to **suggest** as **argument** is to ____________ .

   A possess
   B prevent
   C provoke
   D perceive

3. **Inventor** is to **creative** as **soldier** is to ________ .

   A standard
   B patriotic
   C persuasive
   D dependent

4. **Sleep** is to **gentle** as **toil** is to ____________ .

   A voluntary
   B strenuous
   C seasonal
   D qualified

5. **Arrive** is to **leave** as **entry** is to __________ .

   A gateway
   B residence
   C departure
   D highway

6. **Father** is to **children** as **parent** is to ____________ .

   A offspring
   B forerunner
   C foundation
   D household

7. **Tell** is to **ask** as **notify** is to ____________ .

   A react
   B respond
   C deny
   D query

8. **Sell** is to **producer** as **purchase** is to ____________ .

   A visitor
   B complainer
   C consumer
   D observer

I.E. Choose the correct word to complete an analogy

Comprehension

I. Determine the meaning of words in written texts

A. Use root words and other structural cues to recognize new words
B. Use context clues to determine word meaning
C. Recognize correct meaning of words with multiple meanings
D. Demonstrate knowledge of synonyms and antonyms

II. Identify supporting ideas

A. Identify relevant facts and details
B. Use text structure to locate relevant facts and details
C. Sequence events in chronological order
D. Follow written directions

III. Summarize a variety of written texts

A. Determine the main idea or essential message of a text
B. Summarize the major ideas, themes, or procedures in a text

IV. Perceive relationships and recognize outcomes

A. Identify cause and effect relationships in a text
B. Make and verify predictions with information from a text
C. Connect, compare, and contrast ideas, themes, and issues across texts
D. Respond to texts by making observations/connections, speculating, questioning, etc.

V. Analyze information in order to make inferences and generalizations

A. Make and explain inferences
B. Support interpretations/conclusions with information from a text
C. Make generalizations based on information from a text

VI. Recognize points of view, propaganda, and statements of fact and opinion

A. Distinguish fact from opinion in a text
B. Identify the author's purpose
C. Recognize logical, ethical, and emotional appeals
D. Analyze positions, arguments, and evidence presented by an author
E. Identify bias and propaganda

VII. Read, analyze, and interpret literature

A. Identify genres of fiction, nonfiction, and poetry
B. Identify characteristics representative of a given genre
C. Identify important literary elements
D. Recognize/interpret figurative language

1: Do you know how to study?

If you are like most students, you probably have some questions about the best way to study. You might wonder about the best time to study or how to remember the most important points of a lesson. It is really not hard to study, but there are some ways to make the most of the time spent "hitting the books."

Where and When

Every student needs a place to study. Whether you live in a tiny one-bedroom apartment or a **sprawling** ranch house, you should set aside a study area. It can be a desk in a bedroom or the kitchen table. The place must be fairly quiet with good light.

You also need a set time for studying. You should make a schedule for all your activities. If you have a weekly schedule for chores, work, fun, and studying, you can make better use of your time. Your schedule should be **flexible**. This will give you trade-offs and shifts when necessary.

Getting Started

Begin every study assignment by **previewing** the material. Look ahead to see what's coming—for example, read a chapter's introduction, headings, or summary. This is like looking at a road map. You are making a "mental map" of what is ahead. You complete the map's details as you read the chapter.

Reading and Thinking

As you read the chapter, try to fit details into your mental map. Pause before each new section to "test" your understanding. Use special strategies for learning and remembering. For example, you can ask yourself questions: What conclusions can I draw from this? How should I categorize the information? How does this information compare to what I learned in class? What are the main ideas?

Taking Notes

It is impossible to remember everything you read, but you will remember more if you take notes as you read. These notes serve as a summary of the most important **points**. Taking notes and reviewing them will help you categorize the material, understand it, and remember it. And the notes will help in preparing for tests.

Self-Testing

You should also learn how to test yourself. This lets you see what you know and what you still need to learn. Once you know this, then you can apply your study time more **efficiently**. You can pay more attention to the sections that were your weakest. You can even ask an older family member or a friend to make up test questions for you.

Preparing for Tests

When do you study for tests? Many students think they will forget information unless they do all their studying just before the test. As a result, students usually do most of their studying the night before a test. You might be surprised to learn that there is a better way to prepare for tests. It is actually more effective to space studying over several days or a week. This gives you enough time to understand the material and relate it to what you already know. You should always have time to review material more than once. "Cramming" the night before is not a good idea, and it is more important to get a night's sleep.

All students can **benefit** from following these study steps. Even if you earn straight A's, good habits like these can improve the results of your study time. And if you earn some B's (or C's and D's), you can certainly use these study tips to learn more—and to improve your grades.

Source: This passage includes information from the Office of Educational Research and Improvement, U.S. Department of Education, Washington, D.C.

Context Clues (I.B)

1. What does the word **sprawling** mean in this passage?

   A Very small

   B Old and messy

   C Dark and empty

   D Long and spread out

Structural Cues (I.A)

2. In this passage, the word **flexible** means—

   A changeable

   B rigid

   C useless

   D workable

Structural Cues (I.A)

3. In which word do the letters *pre* mean the same as in **previewing**?

   A Pretty

   B Pressing

   C President

   D Prepaying

Context Clues (I.B)

4. In this passage, the word **efficiently** means—

   A quickly

   B slowly

   C in a productive way

   D in a useless way

Synonyms/Antonyms (II.D)

5. Which word is a SYNONYM for the word **benefit**?

   A Study

   B Gain

   C Follow

   D Remember

Multiple-Meaning Words (II.C)

6. In this passage, the word **points** means—

   A directs

   B marks

   C details

   D sharp ends

Facts/Details (II.A)

7. Which of the following should you have at a study area?

   A Soft chair

   B Good light

   C Road map

   D Practice maps

Sequential Order (II.C)

8. Which of the following should be the first step of studying?

   A Taking notes

   B Testing yourself

   C Cramming for a test

   D Previewing material

Follow Directions (II.D)

9. To remember more of what you read, you should—

A study at a table or desk

B take notes as you read

C get a good night's sleep

D have a flexible schedule

Main Idea (III.A)

10. This passage is mostly about how to—

A earn straight A's

B prepare for tests

C remember difficult material

D improve study time

Cause/Effect (IV.A)

11. You should have a set time for studying because you—

A can make better use of your time

B will remember more of what you study

C can take notes more quickly

D will have more fun when you study

Predictions (IV.B)

12. If you follow the study tips in this passage, you will probably—

A earn all A's on your report card

B have to cram before tests

C accomplish a great deal during study time

D enjoy school more than you did before

Generalizations (V.C)

13. The study method described in this passage appears to be—

A confusing

B unnecessary

C impossible

D systematic

Interpretations/Conclusions (V.B)

14. Your study place should be fairly quiet so you—

A do not bother other people

B can concentrate on your work

C can ask questions out loud

D can take notes

Fact/Opinion (VI.A)

15. Which is an OPINION expressed in this passage?

A It is really not hard to study.

B Taking notes is one method for remembering more of what you read.

C Self-testing is one way to check what you know.

D Everyone needs to study at a desk.

Author's Positions/Arguments (VI.D)

16. When the author states that your schedule should "give you trade-offs and shifts when necessary," she is trying to emphasize that—

A most students don't study enough

B studying is more important than any other activity

C study time should be fit in around other activities

D a student's schedule should include time for many different activities

Text Structure (II.B)

17. Complete the following outline with information from the text.

Do you know how to study?

I. Studying

A. A place to study

B. ______________________________

II. ______________________________

III. Reading and thinking

A. ______________________________

B. Strategies for learning and remembering

IV. Taking Notes

V. ______________________________

VI. Preparing for Tests

A. Spacing study times

B. ______________________________

C. Cramming—not a good idea

Response to Text (IV.D)

18. Suppose you could talk to the author of this passage. What questions would you ask about developing good study habits? Think of two questions not answered by information in the passage. Write the two questions you would ask, and explain why you would ask each one.

2: It's a Bird's Life

In each of the following passages, you will learn something about the behavior of birds.

How do birds learn their songs?

They learn their music by ear! First, some songbird statistics. Every species of bird has a song that's unique. Most Midwestern songbirds sing to attract a mate. In the bird world, it is the male's job to attract the female, so the male songbird does almost all the singing. By caroling a specific song, the bird can make sure it attracts a female of the same **species**.

Songs are such a big part of a bird's survival that baby songbirds such as sparrows, cardinals, and warblers recognize their species' song as soon as they leave the nest. And, these baby birds learn how to sing within the first two to three months of age, mostly by listening to adult birds—especially their neighbors.

Here's what happens. A bird starts out life on its father's territory. In some cases, the bird will start looking for its own place to call home the summer it hatches, even though it is only two or three months old. Where the bird settles down may be some distance from where it was born. By listening to the different males in the new neighborhood, the young songbird **formalizes** the song it sings for life.

The neighbors are such an influence that birds develop regional accents. A cardinal in central Ohio will have a distinctly different sound than its cousins in southern Ohio—and especially cousins from the South!

Why do ducklings follow their mother?

The mother duck doesn't have to order her ducklings to follow her in a **row**. Instead, she gets a little help from nature.

Unlike songbirds that are helpless and completely **dependent** on their parents for food and shelter, ducks, geese, and other waterfowl chicks are fairly developed when they hatch. Most can walk within a few hours. And, the curious duckling might wander off. So, the ducklings imprint on their mom.

Imprint is a term used by biologists and other scientists. It means that very young animals learn by fixing all of their attention on the first thing they see, touch, or feel after they hatch. In mallard ducklings and domestic chicks, imprinting must take place within the first few hours of life.

This unique way of learning keeps the ducklings next to their mother, where she can keep a protective eye on them. Imprinting also helps ducklings recognize their own mother from other adults of the same species. It also helps the ducklings learn who to socialize with and what characteristics to seek out in future mates. That means a mallard will only look to mate with another mallard, which in turn keeps the species alive.

A duckling might imprint on another species—even you—in cartoons and movies. That really can happen in a laboratory setting, but in the wild, **misimprinting** is pretty rare. Momma duck makes sure she's there to see her ducklings hatch!

Why do birds fly in a "V"?

Canada geese—or other water birds such as ducks, pelicans, and cranes—use the distinct "V" formation to get a little lift.

These birds move the air with their wings as they fly and leave a whirl of wind behind them. Each goose, flying a little to the side and rear of the goose ahead of it, rides the draft of air created by the goose in front of it. That way, every bird in the flock except the "lead" goose saves about one-third of its energy by flying in a V-shape. Being leader is the toughest job, so the geese take turns. Sometimes they trade off so often that they fly in long, wavy lines, instead of V's.

Not all birds form this distinct pattern, though. Smaller birds, such as warblers, flock together in a big group. Scientists think they do this for protection from bigger, meat-eating birds looking for a meal. Think about it—it's much harder to pick out one bird from a big group than a little bird cruising along by itself.

Plus, migrating birds all fly different distances and speeds as they travel from one place to another. (Remember, not all birds migrate.) The American golden plover flies directly from the Aleutian Islands in southwest Alaska to Hawaii. The 2,000-plus-mile flight—mostly over water—takes them about 35 hours to complete. But then other birds, who might fly just as fast, take more time to get to their **destinations** because they stop frequently to rest and eat.

This passage reprinted with the permission of The Ohio State University's College of Food, Agricultural, and Environmental Sciences.

Context Clues (I.B)

1. The word **species** refers to—

A male and female birds

B a type or class of animals

C Midwestern songbirds

D baby songbirds

Synonyms/Antonyms (I.D)

2. Which word is a SYNONYM for **formalizes** as it is used in this passage?

A Listens

B Changes

C Sings

D Remembers

Multiple-Meaning Words (I.C)

3. In this passage, the word **row** means—

A argument

B use an oar

C line

D strip

Context Clues (I.B)

4. Baby birds that are **dependent** on their parents—

A leave the nest right after being born

B need their parents' help in order to survive

C always travel in rows

D hatch more slowly than other birds

Structural Cues (I.A)

5. In which word do the letters *mis* mean the same as in **misimprinting?**

A Missing

B Misty

C Mission

D Misjudge

Context Clues (I.B)

6. In this passage, the word **destinations** means—

A islands

B flights

C final places

D migrations

Facts/Details (II.A)

7. When young birds fix all their attention on the first thing they see, scientists call it—

A migrating

B imprinting

C protecting

D formalizing

Main Idea (III.A)

8. The section titled "How do birds learn their songs?" is mostly about—

A why young birds must stay near their parents

B why biologists study the songs of birds

C how and why songbirds learn their songs

D how birds develop accents

Cause/Effect (IV.A)

9. Being the lead goose in the "V" formation is a tough job because—

A other geese do not want to follow the lead goose

B the leader must rely only on its own power

C sometimes the geese fly in long, wavy lines

D the leader has less protection from bigger birds

Connect/Compare/Contrast (IV.C)

10. What is the same about songbirds and geese?

A Both songbirds and geese are completely helpless when they are born.

B Both songbirds and geese learn important behaviors from other birds.

C Both songbirds and geese migrate every year.

D Both songbirds and geese sing to attract mates.

Inferences (V.A)

11. A mallard duckling that does not imprint on its mother might—

A mistake another animal as its mother

B follow its mother wherever she goes

C find it easy to choose a mate

D walk a few hours after hatching

Interpretations/Conclusions (V.B)

12. Based on information in the passage, which of the following is the most reasonable conclusion?

A All birds find it easy to survive on their own.

B Songbirds have a greater chance of survival than other types of birds.

C The survival of some birds depends on their ability to learn from other birds.

D All birds protect themselves by flying in the "V" formation.

Author's Purpose (VI.B)

13. The author probably wrote this passage to—

A prove that most birds have the same behaviors

B explain some interesting bird behaviors

C compare the behavior of birds to the behavior of other animals

D convince readers that ducks, geese, and other waterfowl must be protected

Author's Positions/Arguments (VI.D)

14. Based on information included in this passage, which of the following statements is most reasonable?

A The author seems uninterested in birds and their unique behaviors.

B The author believes that songbirds have a better chance for survival than geese and other waterfowl.

C The author believes that birds have many behaviors that are important to their survival.

D The author believes that the "V" formation provides the best protection for migrating birds.

Figurative Language (VII.D)

15. The author says that songbirds "learn their music by ear." This means that the songbirds—

A have larger ears than other kinds of birds

B sing specific songs from the time they are born

C learn to sing by listening to other birds

D learn to sing within the first two to three months of age

Interpretations/Conclusions (V.B)

16. Think about the information you read in "It's a Bird's Life." In the circle of the diagram, write an important conclusion about birds that you have reached based on information in the text. Complete the diagram by listing facts and details from the text that support your conclusion. List a different fact/detail in each box of the diagram

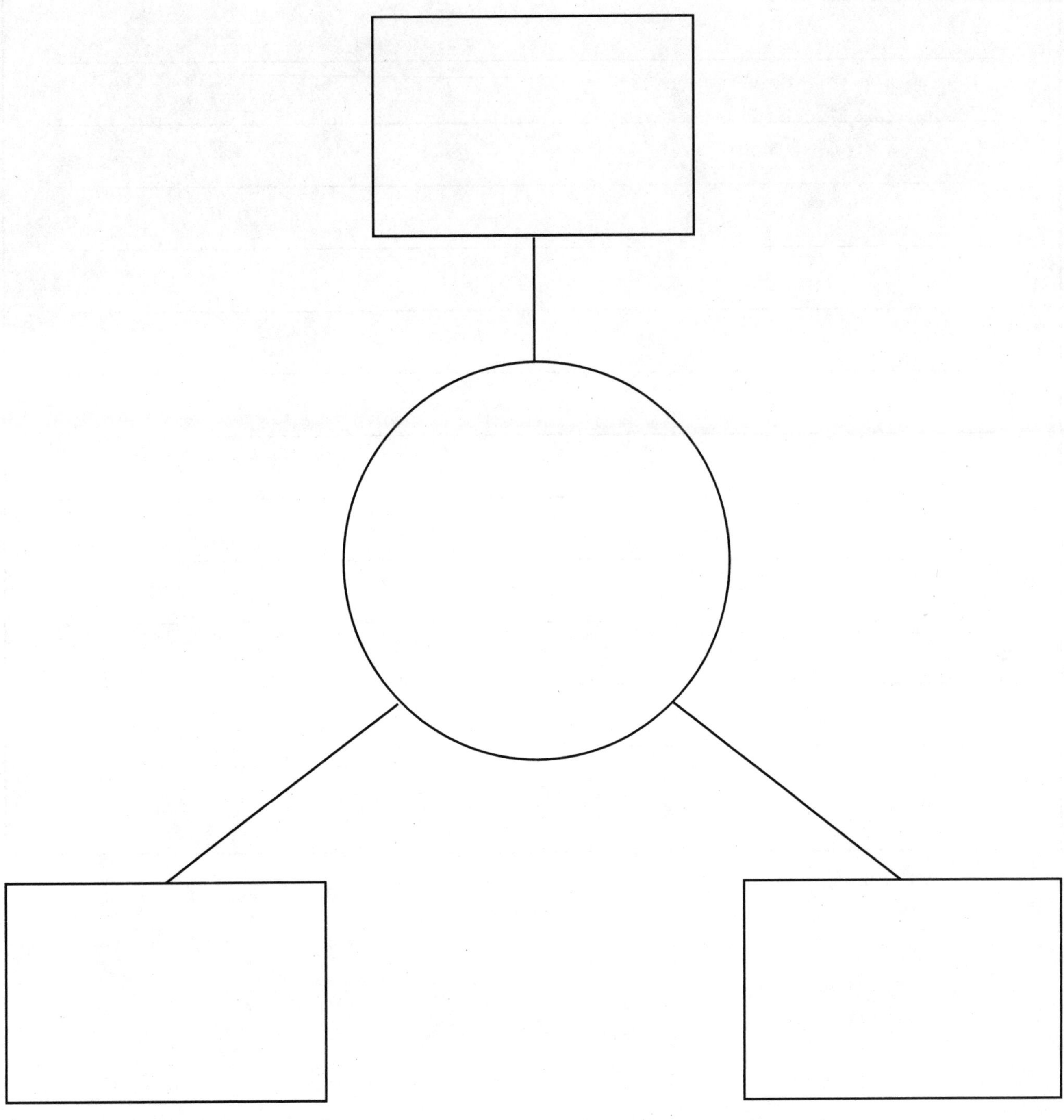

Identify Genre (VII.B); Genre Characteristics (VII.C)

17. Is this passage fiction or nonfiction? How do you know? Use information from the passage in your answer.

3: Y-o-u-u Tom!

You have probably heard of Tom Sawyer or seen a film about this famous character. The following passage is taken from The Adventures of Tom Sawyer *by Mark Twain.*

"Tom!"

No answer.

"Tom!"

No answer.

"What's wrong with that boy, I wonder? You TOM!"

No answer.

The old lady pulled her **spectacles** down and looked over them about the room; then she put them up and looked out under them. She seldom or never looked through them for so small a thing as a boy… She looked perplexed for a moment, and then said, not fiercely, but still loud enough for the furniture to hear:

"Well, I lay if I get hold of you I'll—"

She did not finish, for by this time she was bending down and punching under the bed with the broom, and so she needed breath to punctuate the punches with. She **resurrected** nothing but a cat.

"I never did see the beat of that boy!"

She went to the open door and stood in it and looked out among the tomato vines and weeds that constituted the garden. No Tom. So she lifted up her voice at an angle calculated for distance and shouted:

"Y-o-u-u-u Tom!"

There was a **slight** noise behind her, and she turned just in time to seize a small boy by the slack of his roundabout *(jacket)* and arrest his flight.

"There! I might 'a thought of that closet. What you been doing in there?"

"Nothing."

"Nothing! Look at your hands. And look at your mouth. What is that?

"I don't know, Aunt."

"Well, I know. It's jam—that's what it is. Forty times I've said if you didn't let that jam alone I'd skin you. Hand me that switch."

The switch hovered in the air—

"My! Look behind you, Aunt!"

The old lady whirled round and snatched her skirts out of danger. The lad fled, scrambled up the high board fence, and disappeared over it. His Aunt Polly stood surprised a moment, and then broke into a gentle laugh.

"Hang the boy, can't I never learn anything? Ain't he played me tricks enough like that for me to be looking out for him by this time? … he's my own dead sister's boy, poor thing, and I ain't got the heart to lash him. Every time I let him off, my conscience hurts me so, and every time I hit him, my old heart almost breaks. He'll play hooky this evening, and I'll just be obliged to make him work tomorrow to punish him. It's mighty hard to make him work on Saturdays, when all the boys are having holiday, but he hates work more than he hates anything else …"

Tom did play hooky, and he had a very good time. He got back home barely in time to help Jim, the servant boy, saw the next day's wood and split the **kindlings** before supper—at least he was there in time to tell his adventures to Jim while Jim did three-fourths of the work. Tom's younger brother (or rather half brother) Sid was already through with his part of the work (picking up chips), for he was a quiet boy and had no adventurous, troublesome ways.

While Tom was eating his supper, and stealing sugar as opportunity offered, Aunt Polly asked him questions because she wanted to trap him into damaging confessions. She said:

"Tom, it was middling warm in school, wasn't it?"

"Yes'm."

"Powerful warm, wasn't it?"

"Yes'm."

"Didn't you want to go swimming, Tom?"

A bit of a scare shot through Tom—a touch of uncomfortable **suspicion**. He searched Aunt Polly's face, but it told him nothing. So he said:

"No'm—well, not very much."

The old lady reached out her hand and felt Tom's shirt, and said:

"But you ain't too warm now, though." And it flattered her to know that she had discovered that the shirt was dry without anybody knowing that that was what she had in her mind. But in spite of her, Tom knew where the wind lay, now. So he forestalled what might be the next move:

"Some of us pumped on our heads—mine's damp yet. See?"

Aunt Polly was vexed to think she had overlooked that bit of evidence and missed a trick. Then she had a new **inspiration**.

"Tom, you didn't have to undo your shirt collar where I sewed it, to pump on your head, did you? Unbutton your jacket!"

The trouble vanished out of Tom's face. He opened his jacket. He shirt collar was securely sewed.

"Bother! Well, go 'long with you. I was sure you'd played hooky and been swimming. But I forgive you, Tom. I reckon you're a kind of singed *(burned)* cat, as the saying is—better than you look. This time."

She was half sorry that she'd been wrong and half glad that Tom had stumbled into obedient conduct for once. But Sidney said:

"Well, now, I thought you sewed his collar with white thread, but it's black."

"Why, I did sew it with white! Tom!"

But Tom did not wait for the rest. As he went out the door he said:

"Siddy, I'll lick you for that."

In a safe place, Tom examined two large needles which were thrust into the lapels of his jacket and had thread bound about them—one needle carried white thread and the other black.

He said:

"She'd never have noticed if it hadn't been for Sid. Sometimes she sews with white, and sometimes she sews with black. I wish she'd stick to one or the other—I can't keep the run of 'em. But I bet you I'll lam Sid for that. I'll learn him!"

Context Clues (I.B)

1. **Spectacles** is another word for—

A hats

B furniture

C glasses

D brooms

Context Clues (I.B)

2. In this passage, the word **resurrected** means—

A stirred up

B punched

C breathed

D hid

Synonyms/Antonyms (I.D)

3. Which word is an ANTONYM for **slight**?

A Faint

B Simple

C Distant

D Loud

Context Clues (I.B)

4. The word **kindlings** refers to—

A wood chips

B enjoyable adventures

C small pieces of wood

D servant boys

Structural Cues (I.A)

5. The word **suspicion** comes from the Latin word *suspicio* which means "to suspect." Which of the following words is probably NOT related to the word **suspicion** in meaning?

A Suspense

B Suspicious

C Suspend

D Suspect

Multiple-Meaning Words (I.C)

6. In this passage, the word **inspiration** means—

A taking air into the lungs

B an idea

C a strong influence

D the ability to affect others

Sequential Order (II.B)

7. Tom tells Aunt Polly that he pumped water on his head—

A before helping Jim saw the wood

B before he begins eating his supper

C after Sid tells her about the black thread in Tom's collar

D after she discovers his shirt is dry

Main Idea (III.A)

8. This passage is mostly about—

A an old woman who worries about raising her sister's children

B two brothers who don't get along with one another

C a boy who gets in trouble for playing tricks on his aunt

D a boy who wants to please his aunt

Cause/Effect (IV.A)

9. Why does Aunt Polly ask Tom about how warm it was at school?

A She wants Tom to know that she cares about him.

B Sidney has already told her that Tom played hooky from school.

C She notices that Tom is sweating too much.

D She wants to trick Tom into admitting he played hooky.

Predictions (IV.B)

10. Which of the following is Aunt Polly most likely to do when Tom returns home?

A Offer to sew Tom's collar with white thread instead of black

B Punish Tom for lying and playing hooky from school

C Tell Tom he should help Jim saw more wood

D Make Sidney apologize for getting Tom in trouble

Inferences (V.A)

11. Aunt Polly says that her "old heart almost breaks" when she hits Tom because she—

A knows Tom's actions are making her ill

B thinks she is too old to take care of a young boy like Tom

C feels sorry for Tom because his mother is dead

D wants Tom to feel sorry for her and change the way he acts

Interpretations/Conclusions (V.B)

12. Why is making Tom work on Saturday a good punishment for his bad behavior?

A Aunt Polly can watch him more closely on Saturday.

B Other children will be working for their families, too.

C Aunt Polly feels bad about punishing Tom in any other way.

D Tom will take the punishment more seriously because he hates work.

Generalizations (V.C)

13. Which of the following words would Aunt Polly probably use to describe Tom?

A Serious

B Naughty

C Wicked

D Reliable

Identify Genre (VII.A)

14. This passage is taken from a—

A novel

B biography

C fantasy

D essay

Literary Elements (VII.C)

15. The major conflict in this passage is between—

A Tom and Sid

B Aunt Polly and Sid

C Tom and Aunt Polly

D Tom and Jim

Figurative Language (VII.D)

16. When the author says that "Tom knew where the wind lay, now," he means that Tom knows—

A the weather is going to change

B Aunt Polly suspects that he played hooky

C Sid has told Aunt Polly about the thread in his shirt

D Aunt Polly is worried about it being too hot in school

Literary Elements (VII.C)

17. Select five events from the passage. Write the events in chronological (time) order on the flow chart below. Choose the five events carefully so that you cover the plot revealed in this portion of the story.

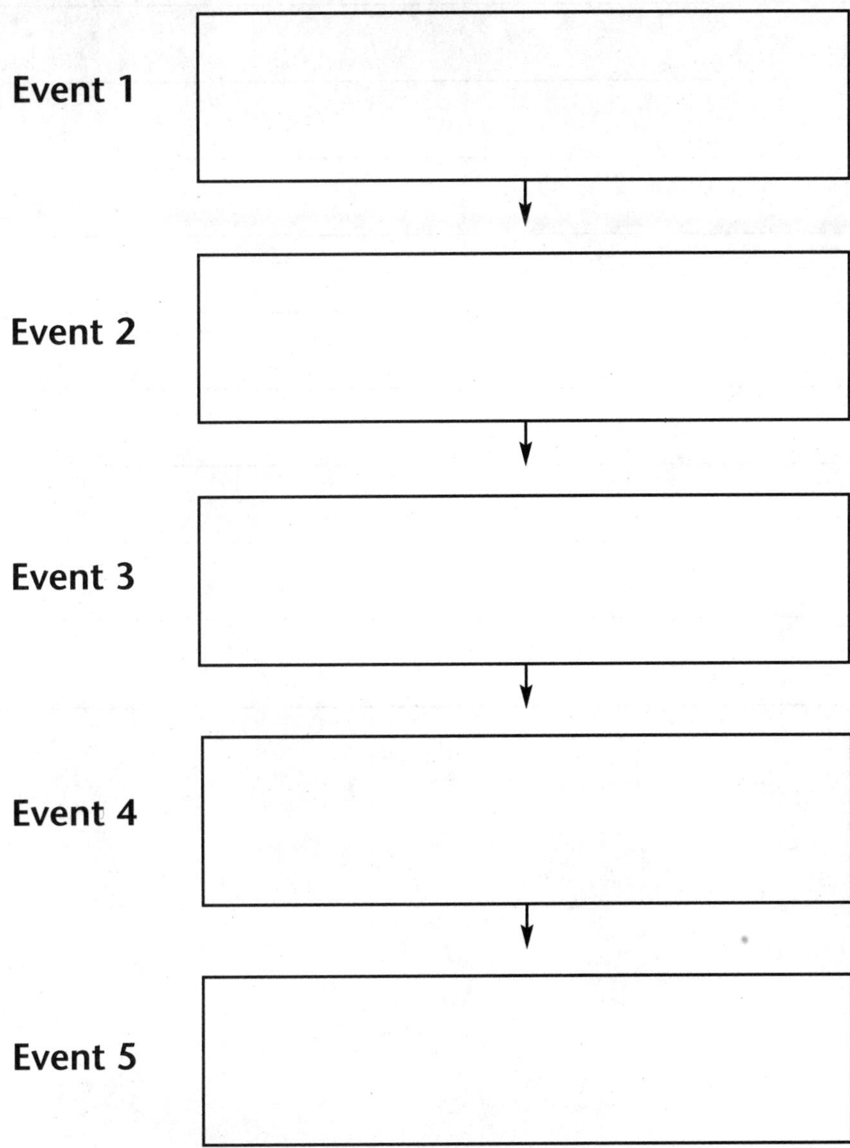

Figurative Language (VII.D)

18. An **idiom** is an expression that does not mean what the words state. For example, "It was raining cats and dogs" means it was raining very hard and has nothing to do with cats or dogs. Find an idiom in the passage and list it below. Then explain what the idiom really means.

Response to Text (IV.D); Literary Elements (VII.C)

19. Recall what happens during supper after Tom plays hooky. Write a brief composition that explains what the author means by this quotation about Aunt Polly: "She was half sorry that she'd been wrong and half glad that Tom had stumbled into obedient control."

4: Cuckoos of the West

When we hear the word cuckoo, we often think of a zany character doing wild and crazy things. That description seems to fit the roadrunner, from the "beep, beep" of the cartoon character to the real-life bird. This New World member of the cuckoo family earned its name from chasing freight wagons and stagecoaches. Even today, the bird is known to chase moving vehicles.

Appearance

The roadrunner is a large ground bird. Even though it can fly, it prefers to run. It has a long, slim build that allows it to run up to 20 miles per hour. Like a hang glider, the roadrunner primarily uses its wings to soar from a high **perch** to a safe spot below. The bird's long neck and bill help it "slice" through the air in **aerodynamic** fashion.

The roadrunner has long legs with four toes, two pointing forward and two pointing backward. Its **unmistakable** footprint forms an X along the sandy ground where it runs. The bird uses its tail, which is as long as its body, to steer itself as it runs. A roadrunner also uses its tail to express feelings, pumping it up and down in excitement.

Black-brown and white **mottled** feathers cover the roadrunner. Its long tail has white along the edges and tip. The under parts of the bird are pale gray. Its distinctive head bears a dark crest of feathers that it raises and lowers frequently. The bird's eyes are a golden color and surrounded by bare skin that is bright blue in front of the eyes. The skin fades to white around the eyes and changes to a bright orange-red behind the eyes.

The roadrunner has a strong, curved beak, which it uses to snap up lizards and snakes. It also uses its bill to make a clacking sound to signal its presence. The bird also hisses and coos to communicate with other roadrunners.

Habitat

Like so many other animals, the roadrunner has markings that blend into its sandy, rocky home in the desert or its grassy surroundings in the scrub desert from Texas to Southern California.

Roadrunners do not migrate. They live mostly in lower **elevations**, although some have been seen in high mountain areas. However, those birds are probably **occasional** visitors rather than permanent residents.

Friendly birds, roadrunners can be easily kept as pets or become regular visitors. One friendly roadrunner once took up residence in a phone booth. It didn't seem to mind the occasional human visitor who came to use the phone.

Diet

A roadrunner will eat almost anything, from quail eggs to hamburger. Because it likes to eat reptiles, especially snakes, it is sometimes called a snakebird. Using a unique method of killing a snake or lizard, a roadrunner beats the prey on the ground or a rock until the animal becomes limp. It is the only bird known to kill and eat rattlesnakes. There are many stories that explain how the bird accomplishes this. According to some reports, the roadrunner uses its beak to stab the rattlesnake behind its head, thus avoiding its poisonous fangs. Generally, however, a roadrunner eats more "bugs" than anything else, with grasshoppers being its most common meal. Roadrunners have been observed jumping three feet into the air to catch the hopping insects.

Family Life

Both the male and female roadrunner take an active role in raising their young. During mating season, the male roadrunner pursues the female of his choice by bringing her feathers, bits of grass, or special snacks. After the pair mate, the female lays four to seven eggs in nests located three to twelve feet above the ground. Roadrunners usually build their nests in trees or bushes, but they also make their homes in barns, carports, horse trailers, desert shacks, and other roadrunners' nests.

The roadrunner's nest is made of mesquite and palo verde sticks and lined with feathers, leaves, and snakeskins. The female lays her eggs over several days, so that the first one hatches just shortly after the last egg is laid. The baby birds help warm the unhatched eggs. When the baby roadrunners hatch, they have no feathers. Their black skin is covered with thin white hairs. By the time they are ready to leave the nest, the young roadrunners look very much like their parents in both markings and size. After the nesting season, the adult birds go their separate ways and live alone until the next year.

Place in Nature

With its undercoat of **down**, the roadrunner can withstand cold and snow. It has a built-in solar heater. On a cold morning, you might see a roadrunner sitting in the sun with its feathers puffed out. In this way, the bird exposes a spot of black skin that soaks up the sun's rays and warms its body. Roadrunners usually live in arid regions with little water. The bird can excrete salt through its nostrils, reducing its need for water.

People pose a serious threat to roadrunners. Because people once believed the birds threatened the quail population, roadrunners were hunted nearly to extinction. Today, we are more enlightened, so the roadrunner population is no longer in danger.

The cocky cartoon bird that keeps Wile E. Coyote in a constant state of upset is not far from the truth. These comical residents of the desert bring a smile to the face of anyone lucky enough to have them as running companions.

Context Clues (I.B)

1. The word **perch** refers to a—

A safe location

B glider

C place to sit

D bird's wings

Structural Cues (I.A)

2. The word **aerodynamic** comes from two Greek words: *dynamikos*, which means "powerful," and *aerios,* which means—

A free

B soaring

C air

D slice

Structural Cues (I.A)

3. The root word of **unmistakable** is—

   A mistaking

   B missing

   C takable

   D take

Synonyms/Antonyms (I.D)

4. Which word is a SYNONYM for **mottled** as it is used in this passage?

   A Clear

   B Feathered

   C Streaked

   D Smooth

Synonyms/Antonyms (I.D)

5. Which word is an ANTONYM for **occasional** as it is used in this passage?

   A Friendly

   B Frequent

   C Unusual

   D Prompt

Multiple-Meaning Words (I.C)

6. In this passage, the word **down** means—

   A swallow

   B toward the ground

   C finished

   D soft feathers

Facts/Details (II.A)

7. According to the passage, which of the following is NOT part of a roadrunner's nest?

   A Feathers

   B Leaves

   C Sand

   D Mesquite sticks

Text Structure (II.B)

8. To read about the colors of a roadrunner's feathers, you would read the section titled—

   A Appearance

   B Habitat

   C Family Life

   D Places in Nature

Cause/Effects (IV.A)

9. A female roadrunner lays her eggs over several days so that—

   A the nest will not become too full

   B some birds will hatch and warm other eggs in the nest

   C some birds will grow at a faster rate than others

   D the baby birds can live alone for awhile

Inferences (V.A)

10. Since roadrunners live alone for much of the year, they probably—

    A eat less food than other kinds of birds

    B lay fewer eggs than other kinds of birds

    C can survive outside of a group

    D are seldom seen by people

Interpretations/Conclusions (V.B)

11. Roadrunners can survive in both hot and cold weather because they—

    A build their nests above the ground

    B eat different types of food

    C can adjust their body temperature according to the weather

    D eat more bugs than anything else

Generalizations (V.C)

12. Which of the following words would the author of this passage probably use to describe roadrunners?

A Dangerous

B Destructive

C Careless

D Entertaining

Fact/Opinion (VI.A)

13. Which of the following is an OPINION expressed in the passage?

A The roadrunner has markings that blend into its sandy, rocky home in the desert.

B Roadrunners bring a smile to the face of anyone lucky enough to have them as running companions.

C The female roadrunner lays her eggs over several days.

D Roadrunners are the only birds known to kill and eat rattlesnakes.

Author's Purpose (VI.B)

14. What is the author's purpose in writing this passage?

A To show why roadrunners are the craziest birds in the desert

B To encourage people to have roadrunners as pets

C To explain and describe the roadrunner's characteristics and behavior

D To entertain readers with stories about roadrunners

Figurative Language (VII.D)

15. The author states that roadrunners "hiss and coo." The words *hiss* and *coo* sound like the sounds made by roadrunners. This is an example of—

A rhyme

B personification

C onomatopoeia

D alliteration

Connect/Compare/Contrast (IV.C)

16. Think of another type of bird. How is a roadrunner similar to this bird? How is a roadrunner different from this bird? Record you ideas on the Venn diagram below.

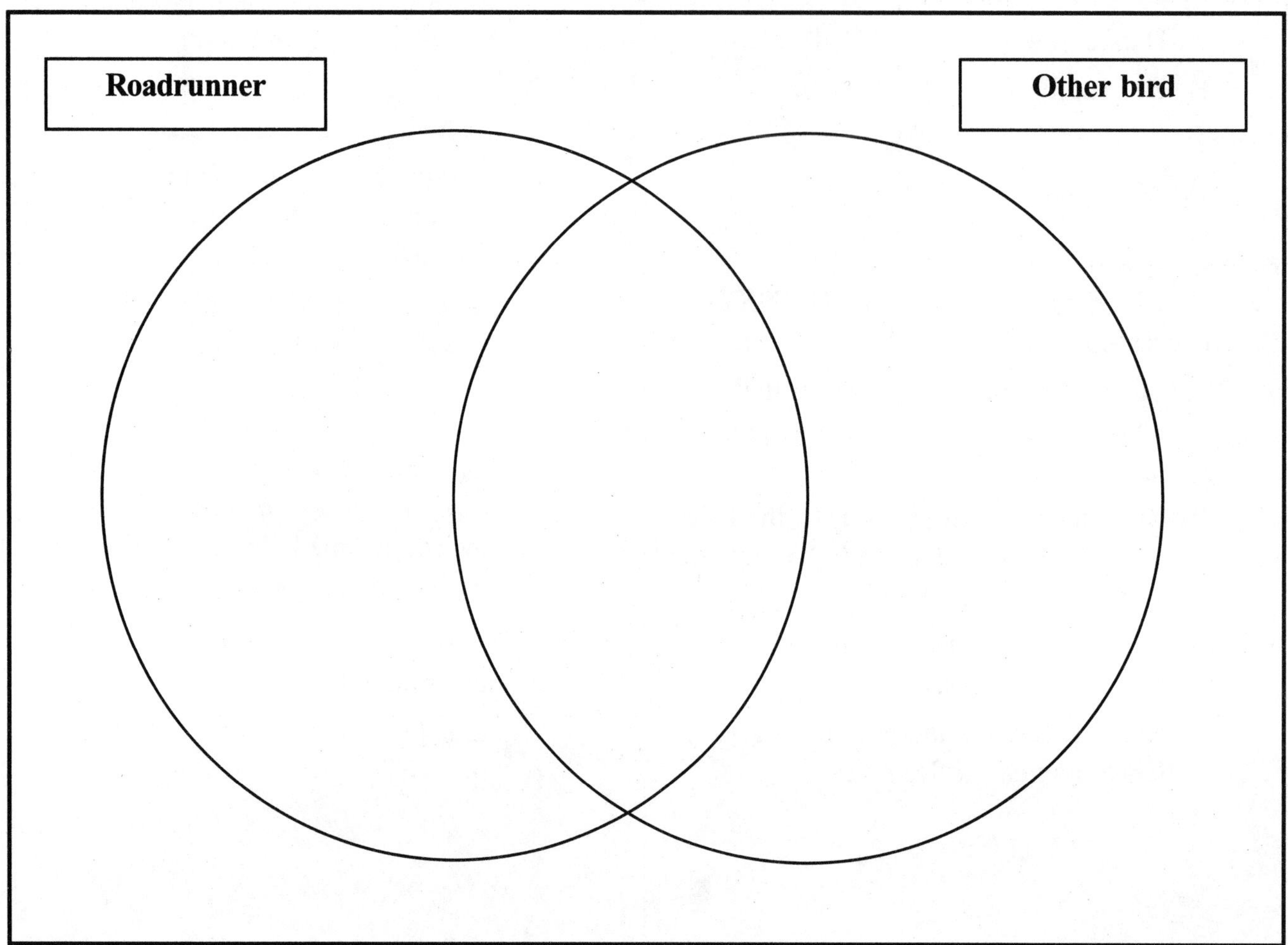

Interpretations/Conclusions (V.B); Facts/Details (II.A)

17. Complete the diagram below by listing facts and details from the passage that support the statement written in the circle.

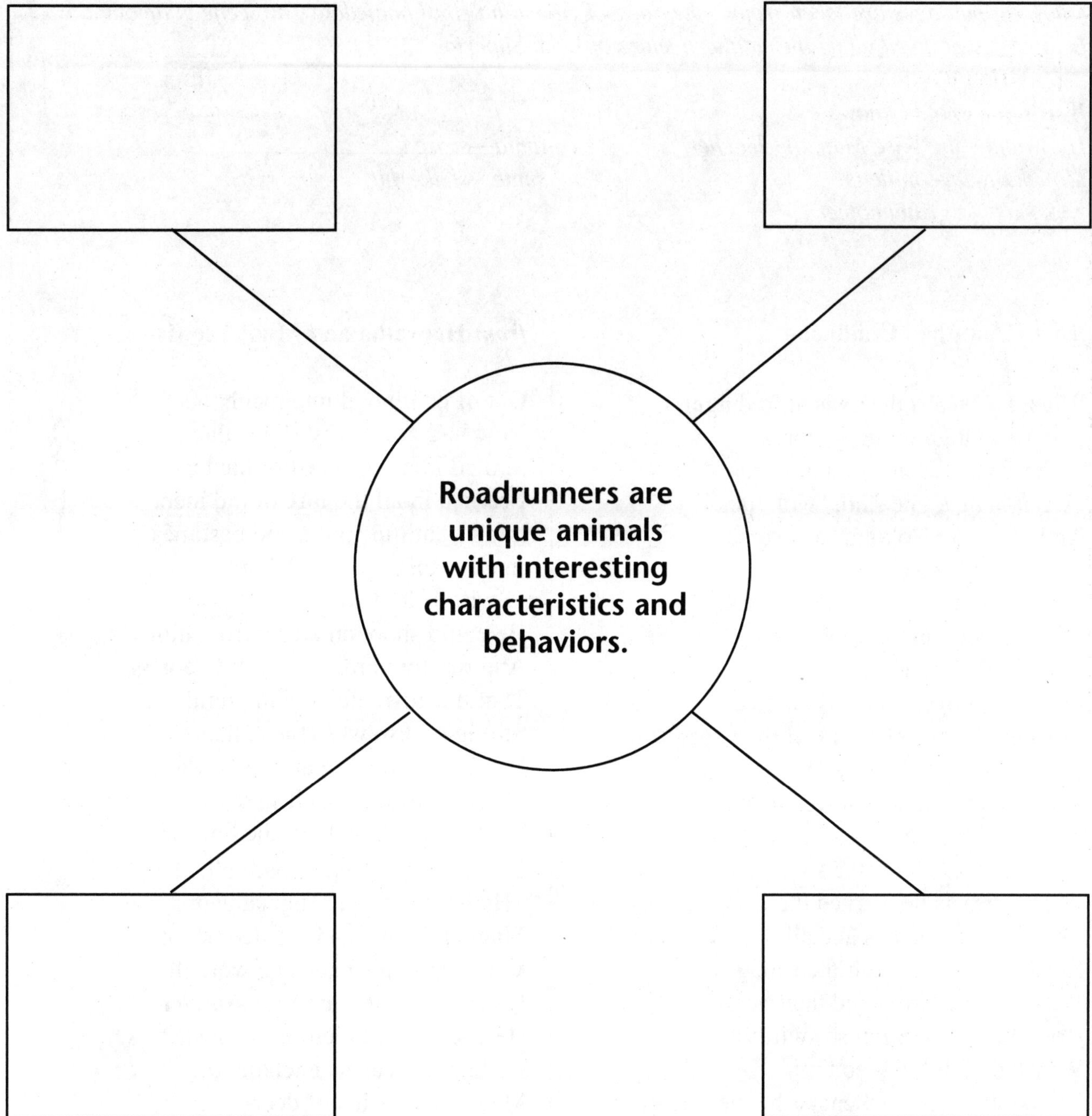

5: The Song of Hiawatha

According to the traditions of many Native American tribes, a Wise Man would come to clear the rivers, forests, and fishing grounds and to teach the arts of peace. Henry Wadsworth Longfellow wrote about this Wise Man (Hiawatha) and the things that happened to him. The following passages are taken from "The Song of Hiawatha" by Longfellow. The scene is among the Ojibways who lived along the southern shore of Lake Superior.

Words you should know:
Hiawatha—the Wise Man, the Teacher
Minjekahwun—mittens
Nokomis—a grandmother
timid—scared
smite—strike, hit

from **Hiawatha's Childhood**

When he* heard the owls at midnight,
Hooting, laughing in the forest,
"What is that?" he cried in terror,
"What is that," he said, "Nokomis?"
And the good Nokomis answered:
"That is but the owl and **owlet**,
Talking in their native language,
Talking, scolding at each other."
Then the little Hiawatha
Learned of every bird its language,
Learned their names and all their secrets,
How they built their nests in Summer,
Where they hid themselves in Winter,
Talked with them whene'er he met them,
Called them "Hiawatha's Chickens."
Of all beasts he learned the language,
Learned their names and all their secrets,
How the beavers built their lodges,
Where the squirrels hid their acorns,
How the reindeer ran so swiftly,
Why the rabbit was so timid,
Talked with them whene'er he met them,
Called them "Hiawatha's Brothers."

*Hiawatha

from **Hiawatha and Mudjekeewis**

Out of childhood into manhood
Now had grown my Hiawatha,
Skilled in all the craft of hunters,
Learned in all the **lore** of old men,
In all youthful sports and pastimes,
In all manly arts and labors.
Swift of foot was Hiawatha;
He could shoot an arrow from him,
And run forward with such **fleetness**,
That the arrow fell behind him!
Strong of arm was Hiawatha;
He could shoot ten arrows upward,
Shoot them with such strength and swiftness,
That the tenth had left the bow-string
Ere* the first to earth had fallen!
He had mittens, Minjekahwun,
Magic mittens made of deer-skin;
When upon his hands he wore them,
He could smite the rocks **asunder**,
He could grind them into powder.
He had moccasins **enchanted**,
Magic moccasins of deer-skin;
When he bound them 'round his ankles,
When upon his feet he tied them,
At each stride a mile he measured!

*before

Structural Cues (I.A)

1. In which word do the letters *let* mean the same as in **owlet**?

A Letters

B Skillet

C Pellet

D Coverlet

Context Clues (I.B)

2. The word **lore** means—

A fear

B knowledge

C arrows

D strength

Synonyms/Antonyms (I.D)

3. Which of the following is a SYNONYM for **fleetness**?

A Anger

B Labor

C Speed

D Strength

Context Clues (I.B)

4. If rocks are hit **asunder**, they are broken—

A quickly

B slowly

C gently

D into pieces

Context Clues (I.B)

5. The word **enchanted** means—

A magical

B swift

C round

D strong

Facts/Details (II.A)

6. What name does Hiawatha give to birds?

A Nokomis

B Hiawatha's Chickens

C Hiawatha's Brothers

D Minjekahwun

Sequential Order (II.C)

7. Hiawatha begins to learn the birds' language—

A after Nokomis explains that the owl and owlet are talking to each other

B before he asks Nokomis about the sounds that birds make

C after he learns to be a hunter

D before he shoots arrows at the birds

Main Idea (III.A)

8. The second passage (Hiawatha and Mudjekeewis) is mostly about—

A a grandmother who teaches her grandson about nature

B the sports and pastimes of Hiawatha's people

C the knowledge and skills Hiawatha has when he is a man

D how Hiawatha learns to speak the animals' language

Cause/Effect (IV.A)

9. In the first passage (Hiawatha's Childhood), Hiawatha is afraid because he—

A wants to talk to the birds and other animals

B cannot find his grandmother, Nokomis

C wants to escape from the reindeer and squirrels

D fears the sound made by the owls

Generalizations (V.C)

10. Which of the following words best describe Hiawatha as a man?

A Timid and fearful

B Wise and capable

C Quiet and slow

D Foolish and weak

Genre Characteristics (VII.B)

11. In which section of the library would Longfellow's "The Song of Hiawatha" most likely be?

A Reference

B Science

C Literature

D History

Figurative Language (VII.D)

12. Nokomis tells Hiawatha that the owl and owlet are "Talking, scolding at each other." This is an example of—

A metaphor

B onomatopoeia

C personification

D idiom

Figurative Language (VII.D)

13. The second passage states that when Hiawatha wears his magic moccasins, "at each stride a mile he measured!" This is an example of—

A hyperbole

B personification

C a pun

D an allusion

Sound Devices (VII.E)

14. In the second passage, the author repeats the **s** sound in this line: "Shoot them with such strength and swiftness." This is an example of—

A rhyme

B rhythm

C alliteration

D meter

Sound Devices (VII.E)

15. In the first passage, Nokomis says the owls are "hooting." The word **hooting** sounds like the sound that owls make. This is an example of—

A alliteration

B rhyme

C idiom

D onomatopoeia

Identify Genre (VII.A); Genre Characteristics (VII.B)

16. Is the "The Song of Hiawatha" fiction, nonfiction, or poetry? Write a brief composition that identifies the passage as fiction, nonfiction, or poetry and explains how you know. Use examples from the text to support your answer.

Literary Elements (VII.C); Connect/Compare/Contrast (IV.C)

17. Hiawatha is the "hero" of Longfellow's "The Story of Hiawatha." How is Hiawatha like heroes in other stories and poems you have read? What qualities of a hero does Hiawatha show? Find examples from the text that show Hiawatha's heroic qualities. Write these examples in the boxes around the circle.

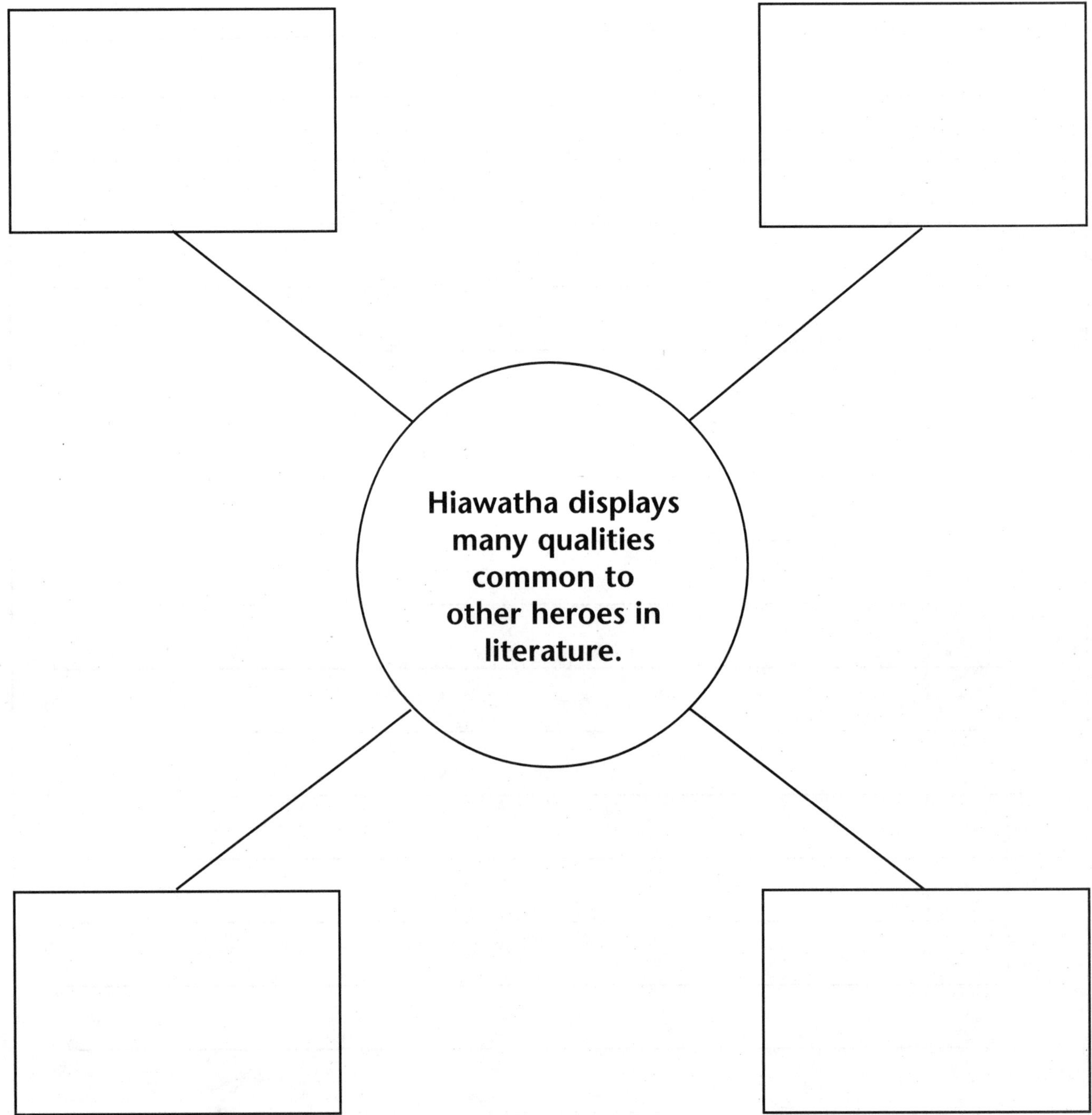

6: A Race for Office

Kathy Jones is a candidate for the state senate. The following article, editorial, and advertisement about her appeared in the local newspaper.

Article

Jones Enters Race for Senate

CLARK—Kathy Jones, a member of the Clark City Council, has announced that she will be a candidate in the upcoming state senate **race**. Jones had hinted at her **candidacy** for several weeks but finally made it official during a speech to local business leaders on Wednesday.

Jones has served on the Clark City Council for eight years. Before winning her council seat, Jones worked on many state political **campaigns**. She also served as an aide to state Senator Vince Jordan for six years. In addition to her political work, Jones has been active in several community service projects, including the Friends of Children Society that works to prevent child abuse.

Jones was born in New Hampshire and moved to Texas more than 20 years ago. She considers herself "a native Texan by choice." She holds a **degree** in elementary education and taught for six years. Jones and her husband, Alan, have three children, ages 6 through 12.

Editorial

A Fresh Voice—A Great Friend

Kathy Jones offers a fresh, new voice for the state senate. She knows how the political system works. As an aide for Senator Vince Jordan, she learned how to make change.

Kathy's leadership on the Clark City Council has helped to build and improve the community. If you enjoy the city's parks and swimming pools, thank Kathy. Without her, you wouldn't have such wonderful **sites** for family outings.

Children in Clark couldn't have a better friend than Kathy Jones. During the past five years, the Friends of Children Society has **established** seven shelters for victims of child abuse. In addition, Kathy's organization publishes outstanding materials aimed at educating parents and teachers about child abuse.

Voters who want change for the better should listen to what Jones has to say. If Jones is elected, Clark will have a good friend in the state senate.

Advertisement

Put Your Good Friend in the Senate!

Like any good friend, Kathy Jones will support your needs and interests.
She has the knowledge and experience to serve you in the state senate.

- Founder and president of the Friends of Children Society
- Aide to Senator Vince Jordan for six years
- Eight years of service on the Clark City Council
- Former elementary-school teacher
- Wife and mother

Vote for Kathy Jones—Your Good Friend—on November 3!

Multiple-Meaning Words (I.C)

1. In these passages, the word **race** refers to —

A people with similar characteristics

B a period of time

C a contest of speed

D a contest for public office

Context Clues (I.B)

2. The word **candidacy** means—

A great victory

B local business

C run for office

D community service

Context Clues (I.B)

3. **Campaigns** are—

A organized efforts to win an office

B decisions to run for office

C service projects

D speeches given by candidates

Multiple-Meaning Words (I.C)

4. In these passages, the word **degree** refers to—

A a person's rank or position

B the general condition of something

C the amount of damage caused from an injury

D a title earned at graduation from college

Synonyms/Antonyms (I.D)

5. Which word is a SYNONYM for **sites**?

A Locations

B Improvements

C Outings

D Leaders

Synonyms/Antonyms (I.D)

6. Which word is an ANTONYM for **established**?

A Created

B Removed

C Predicted

D Published

Facts/Details (II.A)

7. Kathy Jones served on the Clark City Council for—

A 20 years

B 12 years

C 8 years

D 6 years

Paraphrase/Summarize (III.B)

8. Which is the best summary of the ideas presented in the editorial about Kathy Jones?

A Kathy Jones has many reasons for being "a native Texan by choice."

B Working with Senator Jordan taught Kathy Jones how to make changes.

C Kathy Jones' work in the senate and her community work make her a good choice for the state senate.

D Kathy Jones is a good friend to everyone she meets.

Connect/Compare/Contrast (IV.C)

9. Compared to the editorial about Kathy Jones, the newspaper article—

A contains less information about Jones' leadership and work experiences

B makes more statements about Jones that could never be proven

C presents more basic facts and information about Jones' experience and personal life

D explains more clearly why voters should elect Jones to the state senate

Inferences (V.A)

10. From information presented in the editorial, you could conclude that the writer probably—

A has little interest in the election

B believes Jones will be a good state senator

C wants everyone to be Jones' friend

D has known Kathy Jones for many years

Generalizations (V.C)

11. Based on information in the three passages, which of the following words would you use to describe Kathy Jones?

A Friendly

B Intelligent

C Experienced

D Honest

Fact/Opinion (VI.A)

12. Which of the following is an OPINION expressed in these passages?

A Kathy Jones served on the Clark City Council for eight years.

B Jones knows how the political system works.

C Jones is the founder and president of the Friends of Children Society.

D Jones served as an aide to Senator Jordan.

Recognize Author's Appeals (VI.C)

13. The authors of the editorial and advertisement call Kathy Jones a "good friend" because they want readers to—

A feel like they know and like Kathy Jones

B become friends with Kathy Jones

C remember that it is important to be friendly to others

D vote only for friendly people

Author's Positions/Arguments (VI.C)

14. To persuade people to vote for Kathy Jones, the author of the advertisement does NOT include information about Kathy's—

A work experience

B community service

C family life

D personal hobbies

Bias/Propaganda (VI.E)

15. Kathy Jones probably says she is "a native Texan by choice" because she—

A knows voters never trust people from another state

B wants people to know she was not born in Texas

C wants voters to think of her as a Texan

D feels ashamed that she was not born in Texas

Bias/Propaganda (VI.E)

16. Which statement uses the propaganda technique called a "glittering generality"?

A She [Jones] considers herself "a native Texan by choice."

B During the past five years, the Friends of Children Society has established seven shelters for victims of child abuse.

C Jones had hinted at her candidacy for several weeks but finally made it official during a speech to local business leaders on Wednesday.

D Children in Clark couldn't have a better friend than Kathy Jones.

Response to Text (IV.D)

17. Based on the information you read in the three passages, would you vote for Kathy Jones? Why or why not? Write a paragraph stating your position. Use information from the passages to support your stand.

7: The Girl in the Chicken Coop, Part 1

You probably have read or heard about Dorothy and the Wizard of Oz. *The author of that story, L. Frank Baum, actually wrote a series of books about Dorothy and her adventures. The following selection is adapted from one of Baum's books,* Ozma of Oz.

The wind blew hard and joggled the water of the ocean, sending ripples across its surface. Then the wind pushed the edges of the ripples until they became waves and shoved the waves around until they became **billows**. The billows rolled higher than the housetops. Some even rolled as high as the tops of tall trees. The billows seemed like mountains, and the gulfs between the great billows were like deep valleys.

When the wind began to blow, a ship was sailing far out upon the waters. As the waves began to tumble and toss and to grow bigger and bigger, the ship rolled up and down and tipped sidewise—first one way and then the other. It was **jostled** so roughly that even the sailors had to hold **fast** to the ropes and railings to keep themselves from being swept away by the wind or pitched headlong into the sea. The clouds were so thick in the sky that the sunlight couldn't get through them.

The captain of the ship was not afraid. He had seen storms before and had sailed his ship through them in safety. Still, he knew that his passengers would be in danger if they stayed on deck, so he put them all into the cabin. He told them to stay there until the storm was over and to keep brave hearts and not be scared, and all would be well with them.

Among the passengers was a Kansas girl named Dorothy Gale. Dorothy was going with her Uncle Henry to Australia to visit relatives they had never before seen. Uncle Henry was not very well. He had been working so hard on his Kansas farm that his health had given way and left him weak and nervous. So he left Aunt Em at home to watch after the hired men and to take care of the farm while he traveled far away to Australia to visit his cousins and have a good rest.

Dorothy was eager to go with him, and Uncle Henry thought she would be good company and help cheer him up. The little girl was an experienced traveler, for she had once been carried by a cyclone as far away from home as the marvelous Land of Oz. She had many adventures in that strange country before she managed to get back to Kansas again. So she wasn't easily frightened, whatever happened. When the wind began to howl and whistle, and the waves began to tumble and toss, Dorothy didn't mind the uproar the least bit.

"Of course we'll have to stay in the cabin," she said to Uncle Henry and the other passengers, "and keep as quiet as possible until the storm is over. The captain says if we go on deck, we may be blown overboard."

All the passengers huddled up in the dark cabin, listening to the **shrieking** of the storm and the creaking of the masts and rigging and trying not to bump into one another when the ship tipped sidewise.

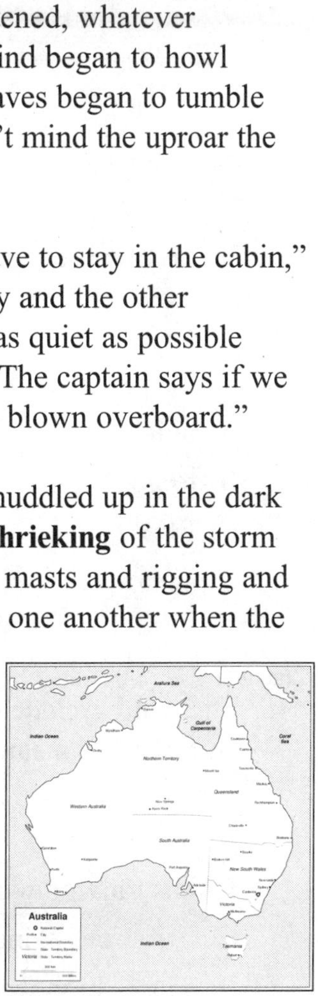

Dorothy had almost fallen asleep when she woke with a start to find that Uncle Henry was missing. She couldn't imagine where he had gone. He was not very strong. She began to worry about him and to fear he might have been careless enough to go on deck. In that case he would be in great danger.

—to be continued

Context Clues (I.B)

1. The word **billows** means—

A oceans

B housetops

C deep valleys

D high waves

Synonyms/Antonyms (I.D)

2. Which word is a SYNONYM for **jostled**?

A Pushed

B Grown

C Sailed

D Stormed

Multiple-Meaning Words (I.C)

3. In this passage, the word **fast** means—

A quick

B to go hungry

C firmly

D smart

Structural Cues (I.A)

4. The word **cyclone** comes from the Greek word *kyklos*, meaning "circle." A **cyclone** is a storm that—

A happens over water

B has rotating winds

C has strong winds

D causes high waves

Context Clues (I.B)

5. What kind of sound do **shrieking** winds make?

A Sharp

B Soft

C Peaceful

D Banging

Facts/Details (II.A)

6. Dorothy and Uncle Henry are traveling to—

A their farm

B Kansas

C Oz

D Australia

Sequential Order (II.C)

7. Look at the boxes below. Which event belongs in the third box?

1	2	3
The wind begins to blow and rock the ship.	The captain puts the passengers in the cabin.	

A Dorothy talks to the passengers about her trip to Oz.

B Uncle Henry leaves the farm and starts off for Australia.

C Dorothy finds that Uncle Henry is missing.

D A cyclone blows the waves over the ship's deck.

Cause/Effect (IV.A)

8. Uncle Henry is weak and nervous because he—

A is afraid of the storm

B does not want to leave Kansas

C has been working too hard on his farm

D has never been to Australia before

Predictions (IV.B)

9. Which of the following is most likely to happen in the next part of this story?

A All the passengers will go on deck and look for Uncle Henry.

B Dorothy will worry about Uncle Henry and go on deck to find him.

C Dorothy will go back to sleep and look for Uncle Henry later.

D Dorothy will write to Aunt Em and tell her Uncle Henry is lost.

Inferences (V.A)

10. The captain is not afraid of the storm because he—

A knows his sailors can handle the ship

B does not know how powerful the storm is

C plans to hide in the cabin with the passengers

D has survived storms like this before

Interpretations/Conclusions (V.B)

11. You can conclude from the passage that Uncle Henry and Dorothy get along with each other because—

A they leave Aunt Em at home to take care of the farm

B they have traveled together before

C the other passengers listen to what Dorothy tells them to do

D Uncle Henry is willing to take Dorothy with him on such a long journey

Generalizations (V.C)

12. Which of the following words best describes Dorothy?

A Careless

B Adventurous

C Cautious

D Sorrowful

Literary Elements (VII.C)

13. From what you have read so far, the protagonist (main character) appears to be—

A Uncle Henry

B the captain of the ship

C Aunt Em

D Dorothy

Literary Elements (VII.C)

14. In this portion of the story, the main conflict seems to be between Dorothy and—

A the stormy sea

B the captain

C Uncle Henry

D the other passengers

Literary Elements (VII.C)

15. Which word best describes the mood (general feeling) of this passage?

A Humorous

B Exciting

C Sorrowful

D Playful

Literary Elements (VII.C)

16. Most of this story takes place—

A in Australia

B on Uncle Henry's farm

C on a stormy ocean

D in the Land of Oz

Figurative Language (VII.D)

17. In the passage, it states that Dorothy "woke with a start." This means Dorothy woke—

A late

B quietly

C suddenly

D loudly

Figurative Language (VII.D)

18. Which of the following lines from the passage includes a simile?

A … the gulfs between the great billows were like deep valleys.

B As the waves began to blow, a ship was sailing far out upon the water.

C The clouds were so thick in the sky that the sunlight couldn't get through them.

D The wind blew hard and joggled the water of the ocean …

Figurative Language (VII.D); Sound Devices (VII.E)

19. In this passage, the author uses colorful language to describe the ocean. Find three examples of the author's use of colorful language. List each example and explain why you chose it as an effective description of the ocean.

8: The Girl in the Chicken Coop, Part II

This passage concludes "The Girl in the Chicken Coop."

In fact, Uncle Henry had gone to lie down in his little sleeping **berth**, but Dorothy did not know that. She only remembered that Aunt Em had **cautioned** her to take good care of her uncle. Dorothy decided to go on deck and find him, in spite of the fact that the **tempest** was now worse than ever, and the ship was plunging in a dreadful manner. Indeed, she found it quite difficult to mount the stairs to the deck. As soon as she got there, the wind struck her so fiercely that it nearly tore away the skirts of her dress. While she held fast to the railing, she peered through the gloom and thought she saw a man clinging to a mast not far away from her. This might be her uncle, so she called as loudly as she could.

"Uncle Henry! Uncle Henry!"

But the wind screeched and howled so madly that she barely heard her own voice. And the man certainly failed to hear her, for he did not move.

Dorothy decided she must go to him, so she dashed forward to where a big square chicken coop had been **lashed** to the deck with ropes. No sooner had she seized onto the slats of the big box where the chickens were kept than the wind, as if enraged because the little girl dared to resist its power, suddenly **redoubled** its fury. With a scream like that of an angry giant, it tore away the ropes that held the coop and lifted it high into the air, with Dorothy still clinging to the slats. Around and over it whirled, this way and that. A few moments later, the coop dropped far away into the sea, where the big waves caught it and slid it uphill to a foaming crest and then downhill into a deep valley.

Dorothy had a good dunking, but she never lost her presence of mind. She held tight to the slats. As soon as she could get the water out of her eyes, she saw that the wind had ripped the cover from the coop. The poor chickens were fluttering away in every direction, being blown by the wind until they looked like feather dusters without handles. The bottom of the coop was made of thick boards, so Dorothy found she was clinging to a sort of raft with sides of slats. After coughing the water out of her throat and getting her breath again, she managed to climb over the slats and stand on the firm, wooden bottom of the coop.

"Why, I've got a ship of my own!" she thought, more amused than frightened at her sudden change of condition. As the coop climbed up to the top of a big wave, she looked eagerly for the ship.

It was far, far away by this time. Perhaps no one on board had yet missed her or knew of her strange adventure. Down into a valley between the waves the coop swept her. When she climbed another crest, the ship looked like a toy boat because it was such a long way off. Soon it entirely disappeared in the gloom. Then Dorothy gave a sigh of regret at parting with Uncle Henry and began to wonder what would happen to her next.

She was tossing on the ocean with nothing to keep her afloat but a miserable wooden chicken coop that had a plank bottom and slatted sides, through which the water constantly splashed and wetted her through to the skin! There was nothing to eat, no fresh water to drink, and no dry clothes to put on.

"Well, I declare!" she exclaimed with a laugh. "You're in a pretty fix, Dorothy Gale, and I haven't the least idea how you're going to get out of it!"

To add to her troubles, the night was now creeping on. The gray clouds overhead changed to inky blackness. But the wind, as if satisfied at last with its mischievous pranks, stopped blowing the ocean and hurried away to another part of the world to blow something else. The waves began to quiet down and behave themselves.

It was lucky for Dorothy that the storm **subsided**. Brave though she was, she might have **perished**. Many children, in her place, would have wept and given way to despair. But because Dorothy had encountered so many adventures and come safely through them, it never occurred to her to be especially afraid. She was wet and uncomfortable, but she managed to recall some of her usual cheerfulness and decided to patiently await whatever her fate might be.

Soon the black clouds rolled away and showed the sky overhead, with a silver moon shining sweetly in the middle of it and little stars winking merrily at Dorothy when she looked their way. The coop did not toss around any more but rode the waves more gently—almost like a cradle rocking—so that the floor where Dorothy stood was no longer swept by water coming through the slats. Being quite exhausted by the excitement of the past few hours, Dorothy decided that sleep would be the best thing to restore her strength and the easiest way to pass the time. The floor was damp, and she was wringing wet. Fortunately this was a warm climate, and she did not feel at all cold.

So she sat down in a corner of the coop, leaned her back against the slats, nodded at the friendly stars before she closed her eyes, and was asleep in half a minute.

Context Clues (I.B)

1. In this passage, the word **berth** refers to—

A a cabin on a ship

B the deck of the ship

C the mast of a ship

D the stairs on a ship

Synonyms/Antonyms (I.D)

2. Which word is a SYNONYM for **cautioned**?

A Remembered

B Demanded

C Warned

D Argued

Synonyms/Antonyms (I.D)

3. Which word is a SYNONYM for **tempest** as it is used in this passage?

A Ship

B Deck

C Storm

D Ocean

Multiple-Meaning Words (I.C)

4. In this passage, the word **lashed** means—

A beaten

B tied

C flung

D jumped out

Synonyms/Antonyms (I.D)

5. Which word is an ANTONYM for **redoubled**?

A Increased

B Repeated

C Resisted

D Decreased

Structural Cues (I.A)

6. The word **subsided** probably came from the Latin word—

A *supportare*, meaning "to carry"

B *super*, meaning "above"

C *subsidere*, meaning "to sink"

D *suspicere*, meaning "to look at"

Context Clues (I.B)

7. In this passage, the word **perished** means—

A recovered

B died

C lost

D beaten

Sequential Order (II.C)

8. Look at the boxes below. Which event belongs in the middle box?

1	2	3
Dorothy goes to the deck to look for Uncle Henry.		Dorothy sees stars winking in the sky above her.

A Dorothy sees a man holding on to the ship's mast.

B Dorothy remembers what Aunt Em told her about taking care of Uncle Henry.

C Dorothy falls asleep in the corner of the chicken coop.

D Dorothy returns to be with the passengers in the cabin.

Inferences (V.A)

9. Aunt Em tells Dorothy to take good care of Uncle Henry because she—

A knows that Uncle Henry knows very little about ships

B does not think it is safe for Uncle Henry to sail to Australia

C knows that Uncle Henry has been weak and sick

D wants to join Dorothy and Uncle Henry when they get to Australia

Interpretions/Conclusions (V.B)

10. Which of the following is the best evidence that Dorothy is brave?

A She remembers what her Aunt Em has told her about taking care of Uncle Henry.

B She wonders what will happen to her next.

C She does not know how she will save herself.

D She remains cheerful after she is washed off the ship on the coop.

Generalizations (V.C)

11. Which of the following best describes Dorothy's feelings at the end of this passage?

A Terrified

B Gloomy

C Accepting

D Helpless

Literary Elements (VII.C)

12. Dorothy probably would not have been washed off the ship if—

A she had remained brave

B the captain had taken better care of her

C the other passengers had been more helpful

D Uncle Henry had told her where he was going

Figurative Language (VII.D)

13. In the passage it states that Dorothy does not lose "her presence of mind." This means that Dorothy—

A does not understand what is happening

B remains calm even when she is in danger

C worries about finding Uncle Henry

D wants to help the other passengers remain safe

Figurative Language (VII.D)

14. Which of the following lines from the passage includes a simile?

A The gray clouds overhead changed to inky blackness.

B The waves began to quiet down and behave themselves.

C With a scream like that of an angry giant …

D Soon the black clouds rolled away and showed the sky overhead …

Figurative Language (VII.D)

15. In the story, Dorothy sees "little stars winking merrily." *Little stars winking merrily* is an example of—

A personification

B a simile

C an idiom

D an allusion

Figurative Language (VII.D)

16. When Dorothy tells herself that she is "in a pretty fix," she means that she—

A does not know how to fix her problem

B does not like being lost on the ocean

C finds herself in a difficult situation

D wants to find Uncle Henry quickly

Figurative Language (VII.D)

17. In the story, Dorothy sees the gray clouds change to "inky blackness." *Inky blackness* is an example of—

A a metaphor

B personification

C alliteration

D exagerration

Response to Text (IV.D)

18. Write a paragraph that explains why you think Dorothy would or would not make a good friend. Use details from the story to support your stand.

Paraphrase/Summarize (III.B)

19. Imagine that a friend asks you what "The Girl in the Chicken Coop" (Parts I and II) is about. What would you tell your friend? Summarize the passage in one paragraph.

9: A Spring Event

The following passages provide information about gathering the sap from trees. Read both passages before answering the questions.

Passage 1

An Indian Sugar Camp

The following passage is adapted from Indian Boyhood *by Charles A. Eastman. Eastman was born on a Minnesota Indian reservation in 1858.*

With the first March thaw, the thoughts of the Indian women from my childhood days turned to the annual sugar making. This task was chiefly followed by the old men and women and the children. The rest of the tribe went out for the spring fur hunt at this season, leaving us at home to make the sugar.

The first and most important of the necessary **utensils** were the huge iron and brass kettles for boiling. Everything else could be made, but these must be bought, begged, or borrowed. A maple tree was felled and a log canoe hollowed out, into which the sap was to be gathered. Little **troughs** of basswood and birch basins were also made to receive the sweet drops as they trickled from the tree.

As soon as these labors were accomplished, we all went to the bark sugar house, which stood in a fine grove of maple trees on the bank of the Minnesota River. We found this hut partially filled with the snows of winter and the **withered** leaves of the previous autumn, and it must be cleared for our use. In the meantime, a tent was pitched outside for a few days' stay. The snow was still deep in the woods, with a solid crust upon which we could easily walk. We usually moved to the sugar house before the sap had actually started.

My grandmother worked like a beaver in these days (or rather like a muskrat, as the Indians say; for this industrious little animal sometimes collects as many as six or eight bushels of roots for the winter, only to be robbed of his store by some of our people). If there was **prospect** of a good sugaring season, she made a second and even a third canoe to contain the sap. These canoes were afterward used by the hunters for their proper purpose.

My grandmother also collected a good supply of fuel for the fires, for she would not have much time to gather wood when the sap began to flow. The month of April brought showers which carried most of the snow off into the Minnesota River. Now the women began to test the trees—moving among them, axe in hand, and striking a single quick blow, to see if the sap would appear. The trees, like people, have their individual characters. Some were ready to give up their life-blood, while others were more **reluctant**. A birch basin was set under each tree, and a hardwood chip was driven deep into the cut which the axe had made. From the corners of this chip—at first drop by drop, then more freely—the sap trickled into the little dishes.

It is usual to make sugar from maple trees, but several other trees were also tapped by the Indians. From the birch and ash was made a dark-colored sugar, with a somewhat bitter taste. This was used for **medicinal** purposes. The box elder yielded a beautiful white sugar, whose only fault was that there was never enough of it!

A long fire was now made in the sugar house. A row of brass kettles was hung over the blaze. The sap was collected by the women in tin or birch buckets and poured into the canoes, from which the kettles were kept filled. The boys' hearts beat high when they heard the welcome hissing sound of the boiling sap! Each boy claimed one kettle for his special charge. It was his duty to see that the fire was kept up under it, to watch lest it boil over, and finally, when the sap became syrup, to test it upon the snow, dipping it out with a wooden paddle.

The first day or two we ate nearly all that could be made. It was not until the sweetness began to fade that my grandmother set herself in earnest to **store** up sugar for future use. She made it into cakes of various forms, in birch molds, and sometimes in hollow canes or reeds, and in the bills of ducks and geese. Some of it was crushed and packed in rawhide cases. Being a smart woman, she did not give it to us after the first month or so, except on special occasions. The smaller candies were saved as a treat for the little fellows, and the sugar was eaten at feasts with wild rice or parched corn, and also with pounded dried meat. Coffee and tea were all unknown to us in those days.

Passage 2

A Sweet, Clear Liquid

Why does sap flow from maple trees? Nobody really knows for sure, but people have been collecting sap—the sweet, clear liquid from maple trees—for centuries. Maple syrup comes from maple sap.

The best time for collecting sap is late winter or early spring. Temperatures then often are above freezing, or 32 degrees F, during the day, but below freezing at night.

People don't completely understand why the changing temperatures cause sap to flow. The best theory is that below-freezing temperatures cause sap to freeze and make gases in the sapwood (that's the wood just under the bark) to squeeze together. This leaves room for more water, which is sucked from the ground and into the sapwood by suction, like when you drink from a straw. This extra water then mixes with the sap already in the tree.

When warm weather returns and the sap melts, there is too much of it to fit in the trees. People drill a hole in the sapwood to catch the extra sap in a bucket. The sap can then be made into enough maple syrup to cover all the pancakes you want!

Passage 2 is reprinted with the permission of The Ohio State University's College of Food, Agricultural, and Environmental Sciences.

Synonyms/Antonyms (I.D)

1. Which word is a SYNONYM for **utensils**?

A Canoes

B Tools

C Trees

D Basins

Context Clues (I.B)

2. The word **troughs** means—

A bowls

B canoes

C drops

D kettles

Context Clues (I.B)

3. **Withered** leaves are—

A fresh

B covered

C sweet

D dry

Structural Cues (I.A)

4. The word **prospect** means "hope." The word **prospect** probably came from the Latin word—

A *probare,* meaning "to prove"

B *prohibere,* meaning "to keep off"

C *proclamare,* meaning "to cry out"

D *prospicere,* meaning "to look forward"

Context Clues (I.B)

5. The word **reluctant** means—

A taller

B reachable

C unwilling

D individual

Structural Cues (I.A)

6. The word **medicinal** comes from the Latin word *medicus*, meaning "doctor." Which of the following words probably comes from the same Latin word?

A Medium

B Medic

C Media

D Medal

Multiple-Meaning Words (I.C)

7. In Passage 1, the word **store** means—

A shop

B value

C supply

D save

Facts/Details (II.A)

8. According to Passage 1, which tree's sap makes a white sugar?

A Maple

B Birch

C Box elder

D Ash

Facts/Details (II.A)

9. According to Passage 2, wood just under the bark of a maple tree is called—

A liquid

B flow

C suction

D sapwood

Sequential Order (II.C)

10. According to Passage 2, people drill a hole in sapwood—

A during the coldest days of the year

B after warm weather returns in spring

C before extra water in the tree mixes with the sap

D right after the temperature falls below 32 degrees F

Sequential Order (II.C)

11. After the Indian women collected sap from the trees, they—

A poured the sap into canoes

B crushed and packed the sugar in cases

C made small candies for treats

D struck the trees with their axes

Main Idea (III.A)

12. "An Indian Sugar Camp" is mostly about—

A how the Indians used syrup for cooking

B which tree sap is best for syrup

C why Indian women were responsible for collecting sap and making syrup and sugar

D how Indian women collected sap and made syrup and sugar

Cause/Effect (IV.A)

13. The boys liked to watch the kettles filled with sap because they—

A knew the women could not do all the work

B could eat syrup as it became ready

C did not want to go hunting with the men

D wanted to keep warm by the fire

Connect/Compare/Contrast (IV.C)

14. According to both passages—

A the best-tasting syrup comes from box elder trees

B making sugar from tree sap takes too much work

C people usually collect sap in the early spring

D collecting sap damages trees

Inferences (V.A)

15. Why didn't Grandmother give the boys sugar after the first month or so?

A The boys were already sick from eating too much sugar.

B She wanted to save most of the sugar to use later.

C She wanted the boys to collect sap so she could make more syrup and sugar.

D There was no sugar left because the boys had eaten it all.

Author's Purpose (VI.B)

16. The author of "A Sweet, Clear Liquid" probably wrote this passage to—

A entertain readers with a story about collecting sap and making syrup

B compare how syrup is made today to how it was made long ago

C convince people to make their own syrup for pancakes

D explain why sap flows from maple trees

Figurative Language (VII.D)

17. Which of the following lines from "An Indian Sugar Camp" includes a simile?

A My grandmother worked like a beaver in these days …

B The boys' hearts beat high when they heard the welcome hissing sound of the boiling sap!

C The smaller candies were saved as a treat for the little fellows …

D The snow was still deep in the woods …

Response to Text (IV.D)

18. Imagine you could talk to Charles Eastman, who wrote "An Indian Sugar Camp." What questions would you ask about collecting sap and making sugar? List three questions you would ask and the reason you would ask each one.

Question	Reason for Question
1.____________________	____________________
____________________	____________________
____________________	____________________
2.____________________	____________________
____________________	____________________
____________________	____________________
3.____________________	____________________
____________________	____________________
____________________	____________________

Follow Directions (II.D)

19. Imagine that you were going to make syrup from sap. What steps would you follow? Using information from the two passages, list the first five steps you would take.

Making Maple Syrup

1. ______________________________

2. ______________________________

3. ______________________________

4. ______________________________

5. ______________________________

10: An Unfortunate Whale

In March 1991, people living near Matagorda Island in Texas were surprised to find a pygmy sperm whale **stranded** on the island's beach. Injured and in distress, the seven-foot-long whale needed help if she was going to survive.

People seldom see pygmy sperm whales along the Texas coast. Although these animals live in warm waters throughout the world, they live deep in the water. This keeps them away from people and land. Unlike other whale species, pygmy sperm whales are not very **social** animals, so we know very little about them. We know that they grow to be about 13 feet long and usually swim rather slowly in pairs or small groups. Their favorite food is squid, but they also eat shrimp, crabs, and fish.

The Marine Mammal Stranding Network is an organization dedicated to helping sea animals that become beached or stranded along the U.S. coastline. Members of this group quickly went to work for the whale stranded on Matagorda Island. They immediately contacted Sea World of Texas in San Antonio and requested help from the marine-animal doctors at the **park**. The Sea World specialists could not make any promises about saving the unfortunate whale. The doctors knew that beached whales are often too sick or injured to save, but they were very willing to try.

Transporting the injured animal to Sea World was a challenge. The U.S. Coast Guard airlifted the whale in a helicopter. Traveling in a stretcher, the whale received water and ice baths on the one-hour trip from the island to Sea World.

When the pygmy sperm whale arrived at Sea World, the marine-animal doctors set to work. They did not want the whale's condition to worsen, so they first worked to **stabilize** the animal. Because the whale had been beached for some time, she had lost important body fluid and was dehydrated. Other injuries only added to her problems. She had a deep gash on her left side and an injured eye. These injuries made it difficult for the whale to swim correctly. She had pneumonia and did not want to eat. The specialists at Sea World also discovered that she had swallowed a plastic bag sometime before beaching herself.

The doctors placed the pygmy sperm whale in a pool of water where she could replace her body fluids. Her injuries made it difficult for the whale to swim in an **upright** position, so the doctors stayed in the pool to help her. Even though the water was only four feet deep, the whale could have drowned if she tipped over. The doctors also treated her wounds and offered her favorite food, squid. At first, she did not want food, but she finally ate about three pounds of squid. The doctors treated her pneumonia with antibiotics.

The doctors worked for more than 36 hours to save the whale's life. They knew from the start that they should not be too **optimistic**, but they still hoped they could save her. Unfortunately, their efforts could not help this very sick and injured whale. Less than 48 hours after she arrived at Sea World, she died.

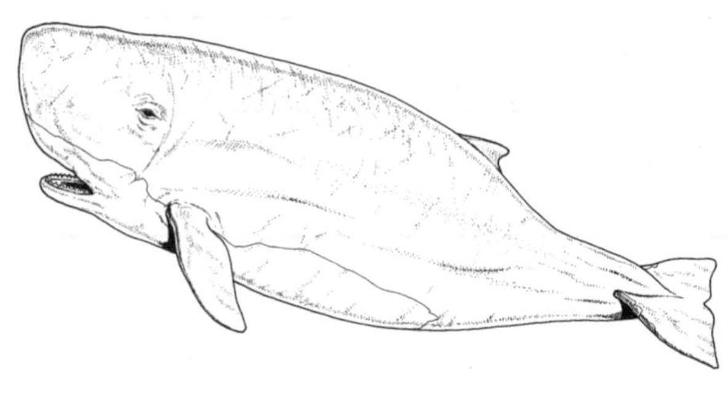

The loss disappointed the doctors who devote their lives to helping animals. If they had known more about pygmy sperm whales, perhaps they could have saved this one. Unfortunately, most of what they knew about this species came from caring for beached or stranded ones. Those animals were usually ill or injured. Taking care of sick or injured animals is not the best way to learn about their natural behaviors and needs.

Context Clues (I.B)

1. The word **stranded** means—

   A friendly

   B run aground

   C surviving

   D dangerous

Structural Cues (I.A)

2. The word **social** comes from the Latin word *socius*, which means "companion." Which of the following words is most closely related in meaning to the word **social**?

   A Scenic

   B Source

   C Science

   D Society

Synonyms/Antonyms (I.D)

3. Which of the following is a SYNONYM for the word **upright**?

   A Treatment

   B Fluid

   C Position

   D Vertical

Context Clues (I.B)

4. The word **optimistic** means—

   A discouraged

   B hopeful

   C unhappy

   D disappointed

Context Clues (I.B)

5. The word **stabilize** means—

   A keep at the same level

   B examine in detail

   C place in water

   D provide food for

Multiple-Meaning Words (I.C)

6. In this passage, the word **park** means—

   A bring to a stop

   B a stadium

   C an open grassy space

   D amusement and recreation area

Sequential Order (II.C)

7. After marine-animal doctors at Sea World said they would try to save the injured whale, the Marine Mammal Stranding Network—

   A fed the injured whale its favorite food

   B walked along the beach and looked for other stranded animals

   C placed the injured whale in a pool of water

   D transported the injured whale to Sea World

Paraphrase/Summarize

8. Which is the best summary of this passage?

- **A** The Marine Mammal Stranding Network helps sea animals beached along the U.S. coastline.
- **B** People living near Matagorda Island have the best chance to see a pygmy sperm whale.
- **C** Members of the Marine Mammal Stranding Network and doctors at Sea World try to rescue a beached pygmy sperm whale.
- **D** Doctors at Sea World learn about pygmy sperm whales by saving those that become stranded on the beach.

Cause/Effect (IV.A)

9. People know very little about pygmy sperm whales because—

- **A** there are few pygmy sperm whales in the ocean
- **B** pygmy sperm whales are not interesting to study
- **C** pygmy sperm whales do not like to be around people
- **D** most pygmy sperm whales live near Matagorda Island

Inferences (V.A)

10. The pygmy sperm whale probably beached herself because—

- **A** her injuries and illness made her weak and unable to swim
- **B** she wanted to be around people who could help her
- **C** this kind of whale beaches itself regularly
- **D** she could find her favorite foods along the beach

Interpretations/Conclusions (V.B)

11. You can tell from the passage that the marine-animal doctors at Sea World—

- **A** knew they could save the stranded whale
- **B** realized that saving the stranded whale would not be easy
- **C** cared very little about saving the stranded whale
- **D** did not know what to do for stranded marine animals

Generalizations (V.C)

12. Which of the these best describes the work of the Marine Mammal Stranding Network and the marine-animal doctors of Sea World?

- **A** Careless
- **B** Unreliable
- **C** Foolish
- **D** Dedicated

Fact/Opinion (VI.A)

13. Which is a FACT expressed in this passage?

- **A** Pygmy sperm whales are the most social of all whales.
- **B** Pygmy sperm whales grow to be about 13 feet long.
- **C** The most difficult part of helping a stranded whale is stabilizing it.
- **D** The doctors at Sea Worls worked too long to save the pygmy sperm whale.

Bias/Propaganda (VI.E)

14. Which word best describes the author's feelings about the beached whale?

A Uninterested

B Critical

C Hopeless

D Sympathetic

Genre Characteristics (VII.B)

15. This passage would most likely appear in—

A an encyclopedia

B a science text book

C a science magazine

D an almanac

Facts/Details (II.B)

16. Complete the diagram below by listing facts and details you learned about pygmy sperm whales by reading this passage.

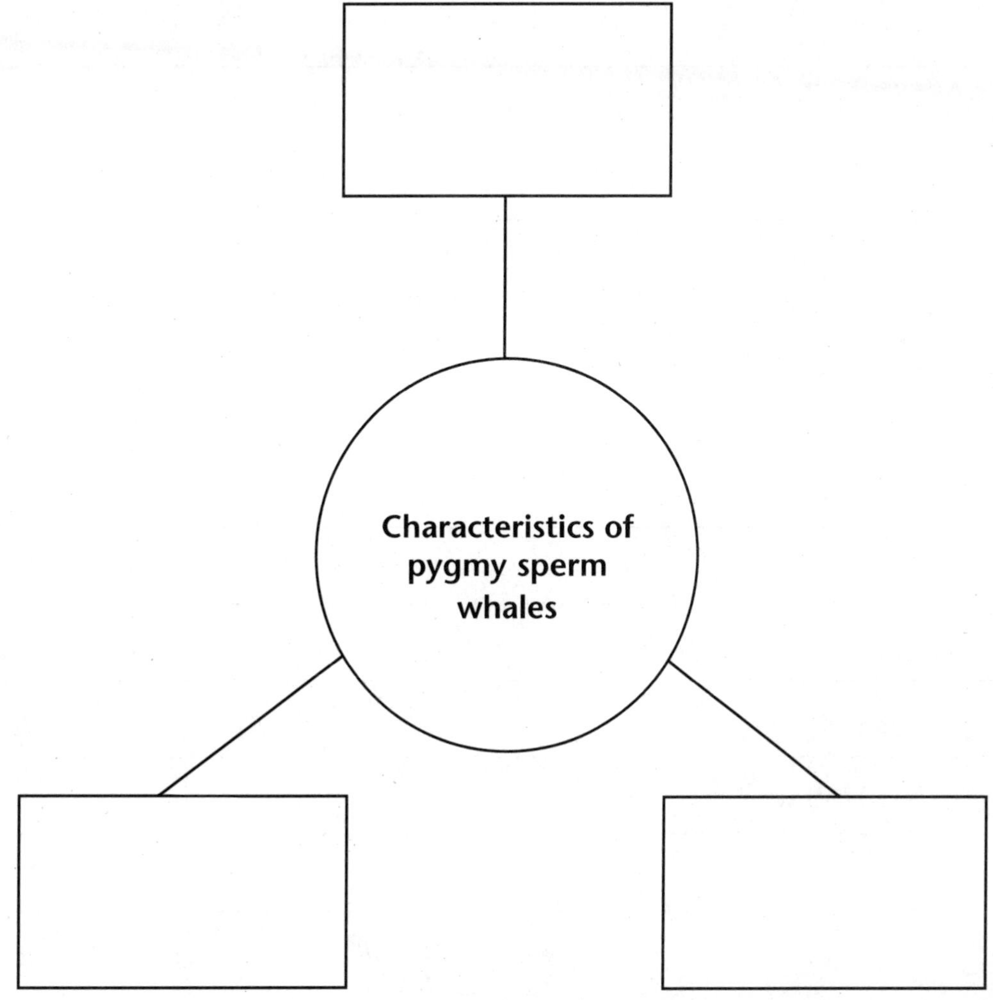

Response to Text (IV.D); Recognize Author's Appeals (VI.C)

17. Write a composition that explains how you feel about the pygmy sperm whale and the problems faced by those who tried to rescue it. Include information from the passage that affected the way you feel about the whale.

11: What Is El Niño?

El Niño is a warm, seasonal ocean current that usually follows a southern route near the coast of Peru in South America. However, every three to five years, El Niño changes its normal pattern. During these times, the current's warm waters stretch farther south than normal. This change in route usually begins around Christmastime. This explains the current's name. In Spanish, the words *El Niño*, mean the "the Christ child."

El Niño and the Food Chain

Many people along the South American coast earn their living by fishing. For good fishing conditions off the coast, there must be many fish like anchovies and sardines. To survive, these fish eat **plankton**. Plankton are small plants and animals that float in the water. They can live only in water that is cool. When El Niño moves farther to the south, it warms waters that are usually cool, so the plankton in that area cannot survive. When the plankton disappear, the fish lose their main source of food and begin to die off. Many birds depend on fish for food. When the fish begin to disappear, the birds must search farther and farther away from their nests for food. Some birds starve to death.

El Niño even affects people. During 1982-83, El Niño reduced fish harvests all along the west coast of North America. The fishing industry suffered and an important food supply shrank. Fishermen, who made their living from catching fish, returned from the sea with empty nets.

El Niño and Weather Patterns

Although many ocean currents affect weather patterns, El Niño has a reputation for creating weather disasters around the world. When water temperatures rise, air temperatures also go up. Higher air temperatures cause more evaporation, so the air becomes heavy with moisture. As a result, heavy rains can fall. During the El Niño of 1982-83, five continents received more rain than normal. Heavy rains in Chile caused **severe** flooding at the same time the west coast of North America experienced dangerous storms. In the United States, serious storms and floods hit both the west coast and states along the Gulf of Mexico.

Oddly enough, El Niño can also cause severe dry spells in some parts of the world. During the 1982-83 El Niño, people in Melbourne, Australia, suffered through a huge dust storm. The storm blew away valuable topsoil, and high winds fanned brush fires. In southern Africa, disease and famine spread during a drought that ruined crops and killed cattle. In India, important rains failed to fall, and the country had a serious drought. "The Child" of 1982-83 was probably one of the most destructive **climatic** events in modern history.

Conclusion

Although El Niño takes its name from an event that many people consider a happy one, it often means disaster for people, animals, and plants. Scientists continue to study El Niño because they want to learn more about its effects on the earth's food **chains** and weather. Someday, they may find a way to predict El Niño's movement or reduce its destructive effects. Until then, El Niño will continue to be an unwelcome guest.

Context Clues (I.B)

1. The word **plankton** refers to—
   - **A** warm waters that flow near Chile
   - **B** small plants and animals that float in the ocean water
   - **C** anchovies and sardines that live in the ocean near South America
   - **D** the earth's food chains

Synonyms/Antonyms (I.D)

2. Which word is an ANTONYM for **severe** as it is used in the passage?
   - **A** Terrible
   - **B** Serious
   - **C** Simple
   - **D** Mild

Structural Cues (I.A)

3. The root word of **climatic** is—
   - **A** classic
   - **B** climb
   - **C** clinic
   - **D** climate

Multiple-Meaning Words (I.C)

4. In this passage, the word **chains** means—
   - **A** metal loops connected together in a bracelet
   - **B** measuring instruments
   - **C** communities of animals that use lower members for food
   - **D** fastens together

Facts/Details (II.A)

5. El Niño's usual southern route is—
   - **A** in the Gulf of Mexico
   - **B** west of Africa
   - **C** near Australia
   - **D** near the coast of Peru

Main Idea (III.A)

6. The second paragraph of this passage is mostly about—
   - **A** why plankton are an important food source
   - **B** El Niño's effect on the earth's food supply
   - **C** El Niño's effect on the fishing industry
   - **D** El Niño's route and effects on the earth

Cause/Effect (IV.A)

7. When El Niño moves too far south, the plankton die because—
   - **A** El Niño's movement keeps plankton from floating in the water
   - **B** plankton cannot survive in El Niño's warm waters
   - **C** El Niño carries too many anchovies and sardines to the south
   - **D** El Niño causes storms that destroy plankton

Predictions (IV.B)

8. In the future, El Niño will most likely—
   - **A** disappear completely within five years
   - **B** destroy all the plankton in the earth's oceans
   - **C** continue to affect the earth's food chain and weather patterns
   - **D** move into the Gulf of Mexico

Interpretations/Conclusions (V.B)

9. It would be helpful if scientists could predict El Niño's movement so—

A people could prepare for the problems El Niño causes

B scientists could prevent the storms caused by El Niño

C dry spells and floods would not happen as often

D scientists could move El Niño in a different direction

Inferences (V.A)

10. Plankton are an important part of the food chain because—

A plankton can only live in the ocean's cool waters

B plankton are important sources of food for people

C other members of the food chain directly or indirectly depend on plankton

D plankton are some of the smallest living things in the food chain

Fact/Opinion (VI.A)

11. Which is a FACT expressed in the passage?

A El Niño is a warm, seasonal current.

B Plankton rely on anchovies and sardines for food

C The first El Niño occurred during the winter of 1991-92.

D El Niño is the most destructive natural event on earth.

Fact/Opinion (VI.A)

12. Which is an OPINION expressed in the passage?

A El Niño can cause both serious floods and severe droughts.

B El Niño of 1982-83 was probably the most destructive climatic event in modern history.

C Scientists continue to study El Niño.

D El Niño usually follows a southern route near Peru.

Text Structure (II.B); Facts/Details (II.A)

13. Imagine that your teacher asked you to read "What Is El Niño?" and take notes as you read. Write three facts and/or details on the note cards below. Make sure the information you list on each card relates to the topic listed on the card.

Note Card 1

How El Niño affects the food chain

Note Card 2

How El Niño affects weather patterns

12: The Indus Civilization

The Indus River begins in present-day Tibet. It flows down through Pakistan and empties into the Arabian Sea. Ancient people settled along the river and used its water to irrigate their land and enrich the soil. As a result, they succeeded in building a great farming society. Their many crops were their source of wealth.

Almost 5,000 years ago, the Indus Civilization began and **flourished** along the Indus River. It spread far beyond the Indus River Valley. It stretched south into present-day India and west nearly to present-day Iran. It included several cities. The two largest cities were Mohenjo-Daro and Harappa. Each city may have had a population of about 20,000.

Discovering the Indus Civilization

The Indus Civilization existed for more than 1,000 years. Yet, for hundreds of years, its remains were buried under layers of dirt. Only an accident brought it to the modern world's attention. In the mid-1800s, the British built a railroad through the area that was once the home of the Indus society. Workers **unearthed** unusual stone seals with unfamiliar writing and pictures of animals. No one paid much attention to the stones at the time. Work on the railroad continued.

In the 1920s, **archaeologists** explored the same area. These scientists study materials left from the past. During their **excavation**, they found many important items left behind by the people of the Indus culture. The scientists found many more stone seals. Unfortunately, they could not **decipher** the seals' strange writing. The messages might have told them more about the Indus Civilization.

Mohenjo-Daro and Harappa

Mohenjo-Daro and Harappa were organized and developed cities. A fort surrounded each city and protected citizens from their enemies. Each city stood atop a high platform made of bricks. The platforms protected the cities from flooding. The cities had streets arranged in blocks, like streets in modern cities. Some of the main streets were more than 30 feet wide.

Houses were made from baked bricks and opened out to a courtyard. Most houses included living areas, as well as a bathroom and a room for the family's well. Houses that had two stories often had balconies. In many houses, drainage systems connected the indoor bathrooms to sewers running under the streets.

Both cities had large **granaries**. These buildings held the city's grain supply. At Mohenjo-Daro, there was also a large brick building called the Great Bath. The city's citizens may have used its pool for baths that were part of religious ceremonies.

Farming and Trade

Many people of the Indus Civilization were successful farmers. They grew many crops, such as barley and wheat. They were probably the first people in the world to grow cotton, their most important crop. They successfully raised sheep, cattle, donkeys, and other livestock.

The Indus Civilization almost certainly had contact with people from distant lands. Among the cities' ruins, scientists found precious stones, minerals, and beads from faraway lands. Items from the Indus Civilization, like pottery samples, have been found in other parts of the world, too. The people of the Indus Civilization must have crossed mountains and seas to trade with others.

What Happened to the Indus Civilization?

The Indus Civilization disappeared around 1500 B.C. No one knows exactly what happened to this great society. In Mohenjo-Daro, scientists found unburied bodies in the streets and stacks of clay missiles along the fort's walls. The missiles may have been used against enemies. For this reason, many researchers believe that the city fell to a sudden enemy invasion. Others believe that terrible flooding destroyed the Indus Civilization. Some researchers think that disease killed most of the people. Still others say that a combination of invasion, natural disaster, and disease probably destroyed the ancient society.

We may never know what happened to the Indus Civilization. The writing on the stone seals may hold the answer, but it remains a mystery to us today. Until someone can decipher the messages, we can only admire the achievements of this great society and wonder about its disappearance.

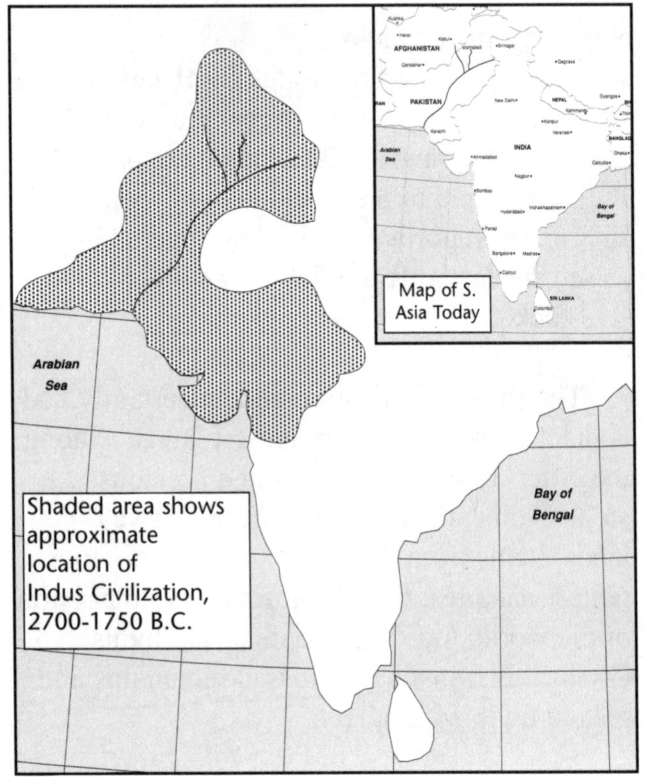

Shaded area shows approximate location of Indus Civilization, 2700-1750 B.C.

Context Clues (I.B)

1. The word **flourished** means—
   - **A** disappeared
   - **B** grew well
   - **C** farmed
   - **D** separated

Structural Cues (I.A)

2. What does the word **unearthed** mean in this passage?
   - **A** Buried under the earth
   - **B** Covered again with earth
   - **C** Made from the earth
   - **D** Brought out of the earth

Context Clues (I.B)

3. **Archaeologists** are scientists who study—
   - **A** the cultures of India
   - **B** unfamiliar writing and pictures
   - **C** stone seals
   - **D** materials left from the ancient past

Context Clues (I.B)

4. The word **excavation** means the—
   - **A** process of digging and removing soil
   - **B** times spent in training
   - **C** period when the Indus culture existed
   - **D** discovery of an ancient culture

Synonyms/Antonyms (I.D)

5. Which of the following words is a SYNONYM for **decipher** as it is used in this passage?
   - **A** Reveal
   - **B** Create
   - **C** Discover
   - **D** Understand

Synonyms/Antonyms (I.D)

6. Which of the following words is a SYNOYNYM for **granaries**?

A Farms

B Storehouses

C Bricks

D Supplies

Facts/Details (II.A)

7. The people of the Indus Civilization were probably the first to grow—

A corn

B barley

C cotton

D wheat

Sequential Order (II.C)

8. The stone seals of the Indus society were first discovered—

A as the British built a railroad in the area

B while the scientists explored the area

C during the first scientific study of the area

D after the discovery of the Great Bath

Main Idea (III.A)

9. This passage is mostly about—

A the importance of scientific study of ancient cultues

B the stone seals discovered near the Indus River

C the importance of farming and trade in the Indus culture

D an ancient civilization that once existed near the Indus River

Cause/Effect (IV.A)

10. Some scientists believe that the Indus Civilization was destroyed by an enemy invasion because—

A most ancient cultures were destroyed by invaders

B the stone seals tell the story of an invasion

C there were clay missiles found along the walls of Mohenjo-Daro

D the people of the Indus Civilization traded with people from other lands

Predictions (IV.B)

11. Based on information you read in this passage, which of the following is most likely to happen?

A Scientists will continue to study the stone seals and try to read the messages on them.

B Scientists will cover the remains of the Indus Civilization with soil to protect them.

C People will rebuild Mohenjo-Daro and Harappa.

D Scientists will lose interest and end their study of the Indus Civilization.

Inferences (V.A)

12. Scientists cannot read the messages written on the stone seals because the messages are—

A in the form of pictures

B carved too deeply in the stones

C written in a language no one uses today

D too old to have any meaning

Generalizations (V.C)

13. The author gives enough information for you to believe that the Indus Civilization was very—

A violent

B strange

C advanced

D dirty

Author's Positions/Arguments (VI.D)

14. The author of the passage gives evidence that the Indus Civilization—

A had no contact with other cultures

B disappeared rather suddenly

C gave little freedom to the people

D built cities that were more modern than today's cities

Author's Positions/Arguments (VI.D)

15. The author seems to believe that the stone seals—

A could reveal many things about the Indus Civilization

B are not as important as scientists believe they are

C caused the disappearance of the Indus Civilization

D came from places far from the Indus River

Recognize Author's Appeals (VI.C)

16. The author states that "only an accident brought it to the modern world's attention" to convince the reader that—

A the British knew about the Indus Civilization for hundreds of years

B the discovery of an ancient culture is usually not planned

C the remains of the Indus culture were difficult to find

D the railroad workers did not know about the Indus Civilization before they began their work

Fact/Opinion (VI.A)

17. Which is an OPINION expressed in the passage?

A Ancient people built a great farming society along the Indus River.

B The Indus Civilization existed for more than 1,000 years.

C The people of the Indus Civilization grew barley, wheat, and cotton.

D Mohenjo-Daro and Harappa had streets arranged in blocks.

Response to Text (IV.D)

18. The author of this passage provides a great deal of information about the Indus Civilization. What else would you like to know about this ancient culture? If you had a chance to talk to the author, what would you ask? Write three questions that you would ask about the Indus culture, and explain why you would like to have each one answered.

Question	Reason for Question
1.______________________________	______________________________
______________________________	______________________________
______________________________	______________________________
2.______________________________	______________________________
______________________________	______________________________
______________________________	______________________________
3.______________________________	______________________________
______________________________	______________________________
______________________________	______________________________

Paraphrase/Summarize (III.B)

19. Summarize this passage in a brief paragraph.

Study Skills

VIII. Identify and use sources of different types of information

A. Use and interpret graphic sources of information
B. Use reference resources and the parts of a book to locate information
C. Recognize and use dictionary skills

Practice 1: Study Skills

Directions: Read each question. Then choose the best answer. On your answer sheet, darken the circle for the correct answer.

Below is part of the table of contents and part of the index from a book about regions of the world. Use both to answer the questions.

Contents

Index

1. On which pages would you find information about forest products from the Amazon rain forest?

A pages 32–33

B pages 33–62

C pages 38–64

D pages 62–64

2. Which unit would deal with the crops produced in the United States and Australia?

A Unit 1

B Unit 2

C Unit 3

D Unit 4

3. Information about foods in India would be found in—

A Unit 1

B Unit 2

C Unit 3

D Unit 5

4. On which pages would you find information about the Sahara Desert?

A pages 74–75

B pages 75–104

C pages 104–107

D pages 107–109

Practice 2: Study Skills

Directions: Read each question. Then choose the best answer. On your answer sheet, darken the circle for the correct answer.

The following passage and chart explain the common Latin abbreviations used on modern prescriptions.

Prescription Symbols*

Latin was the main language of western Europe for hundreds of years. Because everyone understood the language, prescriptions for medicine were written in Latin. Today, however, Latin only appears in the directions for taking medicine. Certain Latin terms and abbreviations have become a kind of medical shorthand. The following chart shows the most common Latin abbreviations used on prescriptions and their meanings.

Common Latin Terms Used on Prescriptions

Latin Term	Abbreviation	Meaning
anti cibum	ac	before meals
bis in die	bid	twice a day
gutta	gt	drop
hora somni	hs	at bedtime
oculus dexter	od	right eye
oculus sinister	os	left eye
per os	po	by mouth
post cibum	pc	after meals
pro re nata	prn	as needed
quaque 3 hora	q3h	every three hours
quaque die	qd	every day
quater in die	qid	four times a day
ter in die	tid	three times a day

*Adapted from FDA Consumer magazine (July-August 1995)

1. Which Latin word means "day"?

A cibum

B quaque

C die

D bis

2. Which Latin phrase indicates that a medicine should be taken at bedtime?

A anti cibum

B hora somni

C post cibum

D ter in die

3. A prescription taken *ter in die* and *post cibum* should be taken—

A twice a day and before meals

B three times a day and at bedtime

C three times a day and after meals

D four times a day as needed

4. Which Latin phrase indicates that a medicine should be taken as needed?

A gutta

B pro re nata

C post cibum

D per os

5. Which abbreviation indicates that a medicine should be taken daily?

A q3h

B qd

C qid

D tid

Practice 3: Study Skills

Directions: Read each question. Then choose the best answer. On your answer sheet, darken the circle for the correct answer.

Julie read about whales in science class. The following diagrams appeared in her science book. Use the information in the diagrams to answer the questions.

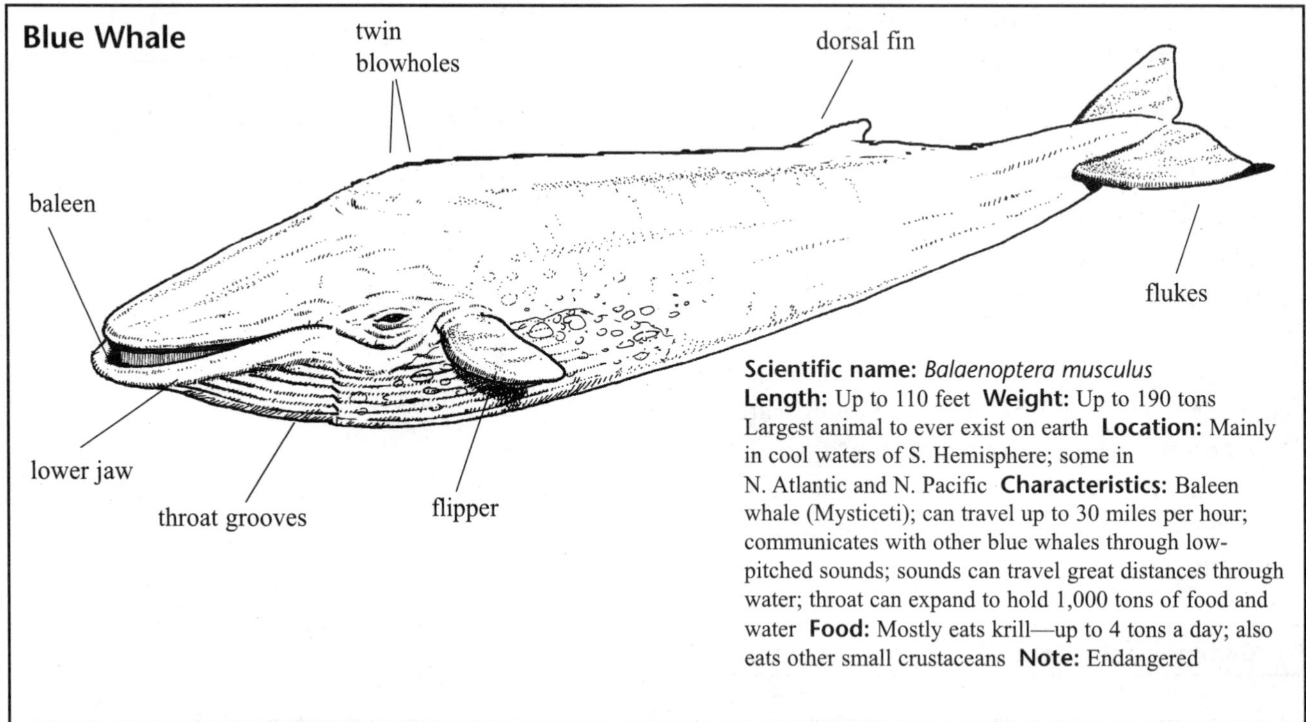

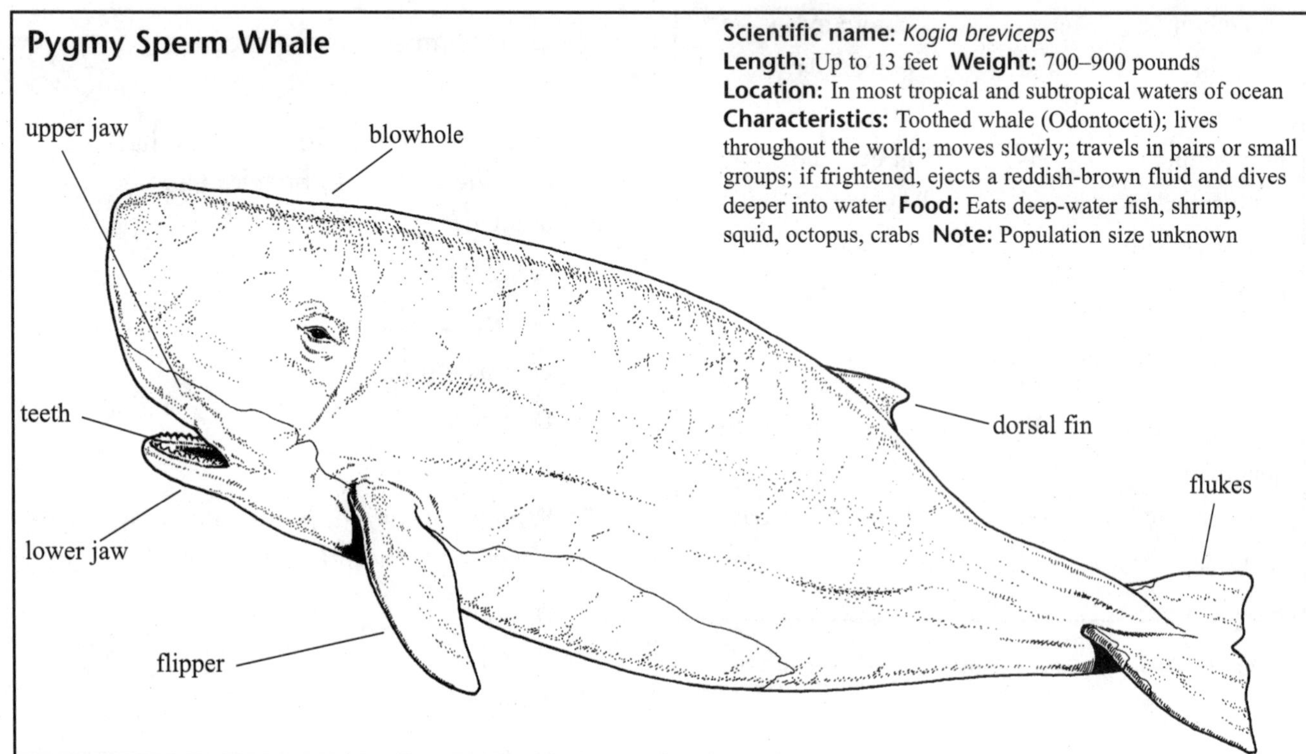

1. Both the blue whale and the pygmy sperm whale—

A have baleen

B are the same size

C live in the same area of the world

D have flukes and flippers

2. Blue whales do NOT—

A have a dorsal fin

B eat squid

C swim in deep water

D use their blowholes

3. Which of the following statements is true?

A Pygmy sperm whales live only in the Southern Hemisphere.

B Blue whales and pygmy sperm whales compete for the same kind of food.

C Blue whales are smaller than pygmy sperm whales.

D Blue whales can communicate in the water.

4. Pygmy sperm whales probably eject the reddish-brown fluid in order to—

A attack other sea animals

B attract other whales

C protect themselves

D get rid of unwanted food

5. According to information in the diagrams, which statement is true?

A Blue whales can store food in their throat.

B Pygmy sperm whales are natural enemies of blue whales.

C Pygmy sperm whales are an endangered species.

D Blue whales usually weigh less than 2,000 pounds.

6. Pygmy sperm whales do NOT have—

A teeth

B a dorsal fin

C jaws

D baleen

7. Which is another name for the blue whale?

A *Kogia breviceps*

B *Odontoceti whales*

C *Balaenoptera musculus*

D *Musculus mysticeti*

8. The whale diagrams do NOT include information about—

A where pygmy sperm whales and blue whales live

B the usual diet for pygmy sperm whales and blue whales

C how the blue whale communicates with other whales

D how many blue whales usually travel together

Practice 4: Study Skills

Directions: Read each question. Then choose the best answer. On your answer sheet, darken the circle for the correct answer.

For his science project, Justin collected information about various types of birds and used the information to make the following chart.

Bird Family	Cuckoos	Woodpeckers	Swifts	Swallows	Shrikes
Family name	*cuculidae*	*picidae*	*apodidae*	*hirundinidae*	*laniidae*
Color	gray-brown backs, white underparts	black, white, red, green, browns, grays, yellow	dark brown, black; can have white on throat	some dull; others blue and green, white underparts	grayish, black-and-white; can be bright red or green
Bill/Beak	long, curved	straight, pointed, strong	small bill; large mouth	small bill; large mouth	hooked, hawk-like
Tail	long; raised and drooped when perching	pointed; stiff for support in hopping up tree trunk	sharp tips on tail feathers	forked	long, pointed
Call/Song	loud call; no song	some with quiet call note; some with loud scream	noisy, screaming	twittering song	unmusical, chattering note; pretty warble
Nesting	low trees, undergrowth	hollowed-out trees	chimneys, hollowed-out trees	barns, cliffs	trees
Habits	solitary, migrate	drill holes in bark to search for food	catch insects as they fly	catch insects as they fly; very graceful	eat field mice, large insects
Examples	yellow-billed cuckoo, black-billed cuckoo	red-headed woodpecker, flicker	chimney swift	barn swallow, tree swallow, purple martin	loggerhead

1. A purple martin is an example of a—

A cuckoo

B woodpecker

C swallow

D shrike

2. According to the chart, which kind of bird has a hooked, hawk-like beak?

A Shrike

B Woodpecker

C Cuckoo

D Swift

3. Swifts build their nests in—

A undergrowth

B barns

C chimneys

D low trees

4. The family name for woodpeckers is—

A *cuculidae*

B *laniidae*

C *apodidae*

D *picidae*

5. Which of the following statements is true?

A Cuckoos have straight, pointed beaks and long tails.

B Swallows have forked tails and small bills.

C Woodpeckers build their nests in barns and eat field mice.

D Shrikes have sharp tail feathers and long, curved bills.

6. Swifts and swallows are similar because both birds—

A have forked tails

B nest in barns and on cliffs

C have white underparts

D catch insects as they fly

7. A flicker is one kind of—

A cuckoo

B woodpecker

C swallow

D shrike

8. Which type of bird uses its tail for support?

A Cuckoo

B Swift

C Woodpecker

D Shrike

9. A woodpecker needs a straight, pointed beak so it can—

A make loud calls

B catch insects as it flies

C eat field mice

D drill holes in tree bark

10. *Hirundinidae* is the family name for—

A cuckoos

B swifts

C swallows

D shrikes

Practice 5: Study Skills

Directions: Read each question. Then choose the best answer. On your answer sheet, darken the circle for the correct answer.

At the library, Norma used the computer card catalog to find books about Charles Eastman. Here are the title cards for three of the books Norma found.

Card 1

973.04975	
Title	Indian boyhood/by Charles A. Eastman; with ill. by E.G. Blumenschein
Author	Eastman, Charles Alexander, 1858–1939
Publisher	Alexandria, VA: Time–Life Books, 1993
Description	viii, 289 p.: color illustrations
Series Title	Native American voices
Notes	Originally published: New York: McClure, Phillips, & Co., 1902.
Subject(s)	Eastman, Charles Alexander, 1858–1939 Childhood and youth.
	Santee Indians social life and customs
	Santee Indians biography

Card 2

Juvenile Biography	
Title	Charles Eastman: physician, reformer, and Native American
Author	Anderson, Peter, 1956–
Publisher	Chicago: Children's Press, c1992
Description	111 p.: illustrated
Series Title	People of distinction biographies
Notes	Includes index
Subject(s)	Eastman, Charles Alexander, 1858–1939
	Civil rights workers
	Santee Indians biography
	Indians of North America biography
	Plains tribes
Format	Juvenile

Card 3

970.00497	
Title	Ohiyesa: Charles Eastman, Santee Sioux/Raymond Wilson.
Author	Wilson, Raymond, 1945–
Publisher	Urbana: University of Illinois Press, c1983
Description	xii, 219 p.: illustrated
Notes	Includes index
Subject(s)	Eastman, Charles Alexander, 1858–1939
	Santee Indians biography

1. Who is the author of *Indian Boyhood*?
   A E.G. Blumenschein
   B Charles A. Eastman
   C Peter Anderson
   D Raymond Wilson

2. *Charles Eastman: Physician, Reformer, and Native American* is one book in a series called—
   A Native American Voices
   B Santee Indians Biographies
   C Children's Press
   D People of Distinction Biographies

3. *Ohiyesa: Charles Eastman, Santee Sioux* was published in—
   A 1858
   B 1939
   C 1945
   D 1983

4. All three books about Charles Eastman—
   A have an index
   B were published in the same year
   C include illustrations
   D include passages written by Eastman himself

5. Charles Eastman was born in—
   A 1858
   B 1902
   C 1939
   D 1945

6. *Indian Boyhood* was first published in—
   A 1993
   B 1939
   C 1902
   D 1858

7. To find other books like *Ohiyesa: Charles Eastman, Santee Sioux*, Norma could look under the following category:
   A physicians
   B childhood and youth
   C Santee Indians biography
   D civil rights workers

8. *Indian Boyhood* does NOT have—
   A illustrations
   B a library call number
   C information about Eastman's youth
   D an index

9. If Norma wants to know what Charles Eastman thought of his childhood and youth, which book would probably be best for her to read?
   A *Ohiyesa: Charles Eastman, Santee Sioux*
   B *Charles Eastman: Physician, Reformer, and Native American*
   C *Indian Boyhood*
   D *Native American Voices*

10. The library call number for *Ohiyesa: Charles Eastman, Santee Sioux* is—
   A 970.00497
   B 973.04975
   C xii.219
   D 1983

Practice 6: Study Skills

Directions: Read each question. Then choose the best answer. On your answer sheet, darken the circle for the correct answer.

The following ads appeared in the classified ad section of the newspaper.

Apartment 2 bedrooms, laundry room. New paint and carpet. Near Lake Monroe on High Point Road. $350 a month. No pets. 555-2345
Apartment 1 bedroom. 1111 Lake Drive, Skyridge area. Near City College. $275 a month. 555-1133
Arts & Crafts Show Sat., Dec. 1, 9am–4pm. 1234 S. Main St. across from Main St. School. Holiday decorations, kitchen gadgets, baskets…Prices for every budget!
Bicycle City Low rider, like new, excellent condition. $200 or best offer. 555-6789
Drum Set Complete with cymbals & stands. $450, or best offer. Call Drum City at 555-1111.
Garage Sale 2222 N. Oak Ave, near Middletown Mall. Fri. & Sat., Dec. 1–2, 10am–5pm. Furniture, refrigerator, stereo, computer, toys, clothes, jewelry, bicycle & more
Office Assistant Jones Law Firm. Need computer & typing skills. Daily hours 8-5, good salary. Near City College. Call 555-4444 for appt. Ask for Ann.
Office Clerk Need computer experience. Must work nights and weekends. $7/hr., good benefits. Apply in person, Johnson Pharmacy, 3333 W. Gate St.
Andy's Dirt Pit Topsoil, sand, & gravel. Daily and weekend delivery. Call 555-1416.

1. A one-bedroom apartment is located—

A near Johnson Pharmacy
B at 222 N. Oak Ave.
C in the Skyridge area
D on High Point Road

2. A person would call 555-4444 to—

A get information about a job
B order children's toys and banks
C make an offer on a drum set
D rent an apartment

3. If Trevor wants a job close to City College, he could apply at—

A Johnson Pharmacy
B Middletown Mall
C Skyridge Apartments
D Jones Law Firm

4. For a part-time job that won't interfere with school, Anna could apply at—

A Andy's Dirt Pit
B Johnson Pharmacy
C Drum City
D Jones Law Firm

5. Mr. Singh could probably find inexpensive gifts for his nieces at—

A Drum City
B Johnson Pharmacy
C Bicycle City
D the Arts & Crafts Show

6. Both office jobs—

A offer flexible hours
B pay the same salary
C require computer experience
D are near City College

7. To apply for the office job at Johnson Pharmacy, Mrs. Wong should—

A write to the owner
B call on the weekend
C ask for $10 per hour
D go to the pharmacy

Practice 7: Study Skills

Directions: Read each question. Then choose the best answer. On your answer sheet, darken the circle for the correct answer.

The chart shows the nutrition information for Rhonda's favorite breakfast.

Nutrition Information
Crunchy Breakfast Treats

Serving Size 1 bar (36g)
Servings per Container 6

Amount Per Serving	
Calories	140
Calories from Fat	45
	% Daily Value*
Total Fat 5g	8%
Saturated Fat 2g	10%
Cholesterol 0mg	0%
Sodium 90mg	4%
Total Carbohydrates 21g	7%
Dietary Fiber Less than 1g	3%
Sugars 9g	
Protein 3g	

Vitamin A	25%	Vitamin C	25%
Calcium	50%	Iron	50%
Vitamin D	25%	Vitamin E	25%
Thiamin	25%	Riboflavin	25%
Niacin	25%	Vitamin B6	15%
Folate	25%	Vitamin B12	15%
Biotin	25%	Pantothenic Acid	15%
Phosphorus	25%	Iodine	20%
Magnesium	25%	Zinc	Trace
Copper	10%		

* Based on 2,000-calorie daily diet.

1. How much protein is in each bar of Crunchy Breakfast Treats?

A 140g
B 45g
C 25g
D 3g

2. How many bars of Cruncy Breakfast Treats are in each box?

A 36
B 30
C 6
D 1

3. To get all the calcium and iron she needs in one day, how many bars of Crunchy Breakfast Treats would Norma need to eat?

A 5
B 4
C 2
D 1

4. How many calories come from fat in each bar of Crunchy Breakfast Treats?

A 185
B 145
C 95
D 45

5. One bar of Crunchy Breakfast Treats is not a significant source of—

A iron
B zinc
C vitamin E
D magnesium

Practice 8: Study Skills

Directions: Read each question. Then choose the best answer. On your answer sheet, darken the circle for the correct answer.

Here are the dictionary entries for several words. Use them to answer the questions.

plumb [plum] *noun* [fr. Latin *plumbum*, lead] a weight on the end of a line, used to measure the depth of water. —*adverb*, in a vertical line. —*adjective*, exactly vertical. —*verb*, **1.** to measure the depth of water with a plumb **2.** to seal with lead

plume [plo͞om] *noun* [fr. Latin *pluma,* small soft feather, down] the feather of a bird

plumose [plo͞o mōs′] *adjective* [fr. Latin *pluma,* feather] **1.** having feathers; feathered **2.** like a plume; feathery. —*adverb*, plumosely. —*noun*, plumosity

plump [plump] *adjective* [fr. German *plomp,* blunt, thick] **1.** full in form; chubby **2.** large, ample: *a plump raise in pay*. —verb, **1.** to make full in form: *plump the pillow* **2.** to become chubby or round: *She plumped up over the holidays*.

1. Which of the following words rhymes with **plume**?

A drum

B broom

C come

D fume

2. Which word comes from the Latin word for "lead"?

A plump

B plumose

C plume

D plumb

3. Which word correctly completes the following sentence?

I asked the hotel maid to ___________ *the pillows before leaving the room.*

A plumb

B plumose

C plump

D plume

4. In the following sentence, which part of speech is the word **plumb**?

The sailor used the line to ***plumb*** *the ocean's depth.*

A adjective

B noun

C verb

D adverb

5. Which of the following words does NOT have a Latin root?

A plumb

B plume

C plumosely

D plump

6. Which two words are most closely related in meaning?

A plumb and plume

B plume and plumose

C plumb and plump

D plume and plump

Practice 9: Study Skills

Directions: Read each question. Then choose the best answer. On your answer sheet, darken the circle for the correct answer.

Which reference tool would be best for finding each of the following kinds of information?

1. The origin of the word *flower*

A *Bartlett's Familiar Quotations*

B *The American Heritage Dictionary*

C *Collier's Encyclopedia*

D *Writer's Guide of Style and Usage*

2. Thomas Jefferson's words about freedom

A *The American Heritage Dictionary*

B *Facts on File Visual Dictionary*

C *Roget's International Thesaurus*

D *Bartlett's Familiar Quotations*

3. The population of India in 1970

A *The American Heritage Dictionary*

B *Collier's Encyclopedia*

C *The World Almanac*

D *The Encyclopedia of Nature*

4. The correct pronunciation of *gracious*

A *Collier's Encyclopedia*

B *Writer's Guide of Style and Usage*

C *The American Heritage Dictionary*

D *Roget's International Thesaurus*

5. The habitat of the American eagle

A *The World Almanac*

B *The Encyclopedia of Nature*

C *Writer's Guide of Style and Usage*

D *Merriam-Webster's Dictionary*

6. The year of Mark Twain's death

A *World Authors, 1900–1950*

B *The World Atlas*

C *Facts on File Visual Dictionary*

D *Writer's Guide of Style and Usage*

7. Facts about famous baseball players

A *The World Almanac*

B *Notable Twentieth Century Scientists*

C *Biographical Dictionary of American Sports*

D *The World Atlas*

8. A picture showing each part of a jet

A *The World Almanac*

B *Facts on File Visual Dicitonary*

C *The American Heritage Dictionary*

D *The World Atlas*

9. Major rivers and lakes in Russia

A *Merriam-Webster's Dictionary*

B *The Encyclopedia of Nature*

C *The World Atlas*

D *Dictionary of American History*

10. Synonyms and antonyms for *bravery*

A *Bartlett's Familiar Quotations*

B *Roget's International Thesaurus*

C *Facts on File Visual Dictionary*

D *Writer's Guide of Style and Usage*

Practice 10: Study Skills

Directions: Read each question. Then choose the best answer. On your answer sheet, darken the circle for the correct answer.

Which magazine would be best for finding information about each of the following topics?

1. Investing in the stock market

A *Popular Mechanics*
B *Reader's Digest*
C *Computer Digest*
D *Business Week*

2. Ideas for decorating a bedroom

A *Newsweek*
B *Home and Garden*
C *People*
D *Reader's Digest*

3. Planning a fishing trip to another state

A *Sports Illustrated*
B *Popular Mechanics*
C *Field and Stream*
D *National Geographic*

4. Last week's World Conference on Peace

A *National Geographic*
B *Highlights for Children*
C *Reader's Digest*
D *Newsweek*

5. Puzzles and games for a 4-year-old child

A *Home and Garden*
B *Highlights for Children*
C *Reader's Digest*
D *Field and Stream*

6. The best kind of oil for your dad's car

A *Business Week*
B *Home and Garden*
C *Field and Stream*
D *Popular Mechanics*

7. The Russian culture

A *Newsweek*
B *National Geographic*
C *Highlights for Children*
D *Business Week*

8. Movie stars and other famous people

A *Reader's Digest*
B *Newsweek*
C *Business Week*
D *People*

9. Best football plays from last week

A *Newsweek*
B *Sports Illustrated*
C *Reader's Digest*
D *Field and Stream*

10. Flowers that can grow in rock gardens

A *Field and Stream*
B *Highlights for Children*
C *Popular Mechanics*
D *Home and Garden*

Practice 11: Study Skills

Directions: Read each question. Then choose the best answer. On your answer sheet, darken the circle for the correct answer.

The Birdwatching Society keeps records of bird sightings at Skylark Lake. The graph shows the number of owls, hawks, and herons sighted in April of five different years.

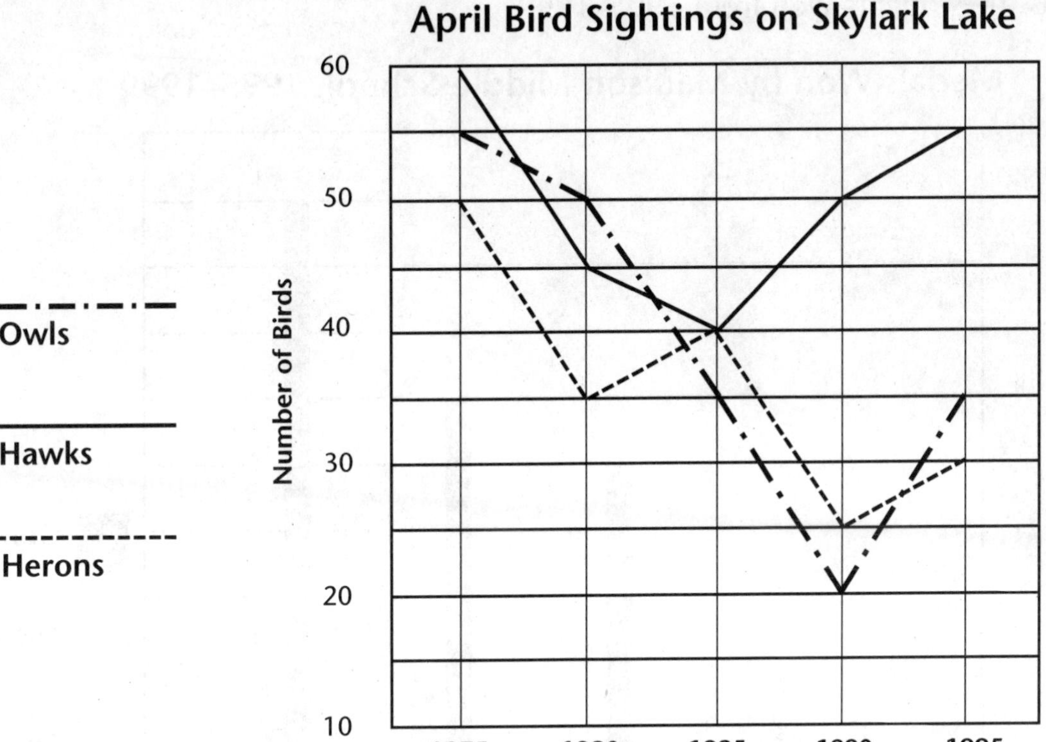

1. From 1975 to 1980, sightings for owls, hawks, and herons—
   A remained the same
   B increased sharply
   C increased slightly
   D decreased

2. Which is a true statement about 1985?
   A More hawks than owls were sighted.
   B The same number of hawks and owls were sighted.
   C Sightings of hawks increased from 1980.
   D Sightings for owls, hawks, and herons increased from 1980

3. Which is a true statement about 1995?
   A Sightings for owls, hawks, and herons decreased from 1990.
   B Sightings for owls, hawks, and herons remained the same as in 1990.
   C Sightings for hawks were the same as in 1975.
   D Sightings for owls were the same as they were in 1985.

4. From 1980 through 1995, sightings of hawks—
   A remained the same
   B decreased steadily
   C first decreased, then increased
   D increased steadily

Practice 12: Study Skills

Directions: Read each question. Then choose the best answer. On your answer sheet, darken the circle for the correct answer.

Ms. Wong, the principal at Madison Middle School, records the number of medals students from the school win at the spring academic meet. The graph shows the number of medals the students won from 1995–1999.

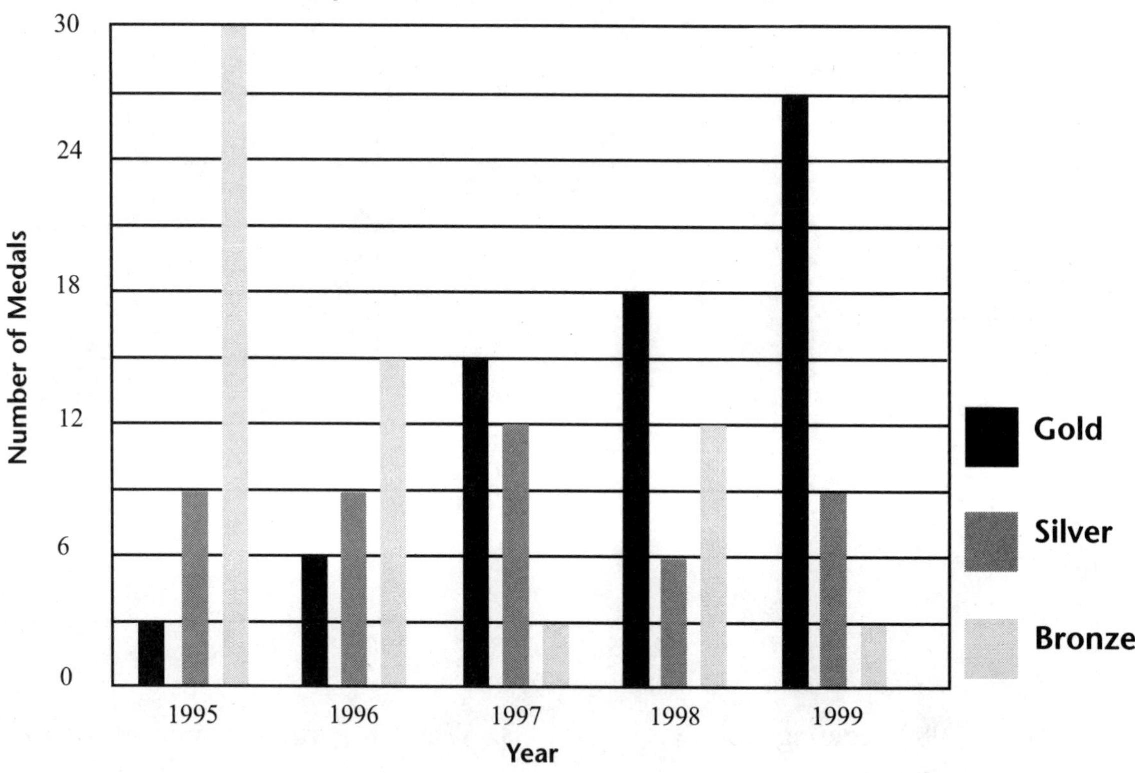

1. From 1995-1999, the number of gold medals won by Madison Middle School—
   - **A** remained the same
   - **B** declined steadily
   - **C** increased steadily
   - **D** went up and down

2. Madison Middle School won the greatest number of medals in—
   - **A** 1999
   - **B** 1998
   - **C** 1997
   - **D** 1995

3. In which years did Madison Middle School win the same number of medals?
   - **A** 1995 and 1996
   - **B** 1996 and 1997
   - **C** 1997 and 1998
   - **D** 1998 and 1999

4. In which year did Madison Middle School win the greatest number of gold medals?
   - **A** 1995
   - **B** 1997
   - **C** 1998
   - **D** 1999

5. In which year did Madison Middle School win exactly 3 more gold medals than silver medals?
   - **A** 1998
   - **B** 1997
   - **C** 1996
   - **D** 1995

6. In which year did Madison Middle School win the fewest number of gold medals?
   - **A** 1995
   - **B** 1996
   - **C** 1997
   - **D** 1998

7. Based on information in the graph, which of the following statements is a reasonable conclusion?
   - **A** Madison Middle School performed better than all other schools at the 1999 academic meet.
   - **B** Madison Middle School performed worse than all other schools at the 1995 academic meet.
   - **C** Madison Middle School improved its performance from 1995 to 1999.
   - **D** More Madison Middle School students participated in the academic meet in 1999 than in 1995.

Practice 13: Study Skills

Directions: Look at the map of Australia. Read each question and choose the best answer. On your answer sheet, darken the circle for the correct answer.

1. The national capital of Australia is—
   A Sydney
   B New South Wales
   C Canberra
   D Perth

2. Which of the following is NOT a state in Australia?
   A Queensland
   B New South Wales
   C Victoria
   D Melbourne

3. The smallest state or territory in Australia appears to be—
   A South Australia
   B Tasmania
   C New South Wales
   D Queensland

4. Townsville is a port city on the—
   A Indian Ocean
   B Arafura Sea
   C Gulf of Carpentaria
   D Coral Sea

5. What is the approximate distance between Melbourne and New Castle?
   A 50 miles
   B 500 miles
   C 1500 miles
   D 2000 miles

6. What is the approximate distance between Derby and Wyndam?
   A 50 km
   B 100 km
   C 200 km
   D 500 km

7. What is the approximate distance between Port Augusta and Brisbane?
   A 500 miles
   B 1000 miles
   C 2000 miles
   D 3000 miles

8. Which city is northwest of Bourke?
   A Brisbane
   B Alice Springs
   C Port Augusta
   D Melbourne

9. Ayers Rock is in—
   A Western Australia
   B Alice Springs
   C Northern Territory
   D Queensland

10. Which city is more than 1000 miles from Sydney?
   A Canberra
   B Brisbane
   C Port Augusta
   D Cooktown

Practice 14: Study Skills

Directions: Look at the map which shows part of Detroit, Michigan. Read each question and choose the best answer. On your answer sheet, darken the circle for the correct answer.

1. Tiger Stadium is located on—
   - **A** Ford Road
   - **B** Gradiot Avenue
   - **C** Michigan Avenue
   - **D** Grand River Avenue

2. On this map, Grand River Avenue appears to run—
   - **A** east and west
   - **B** north and south
   - **C** northwest to southeast
   - **D** northeast to southwest

3. Which road or street appears to run through part of Highland Park?
   - **A** Highway 75
   - **B** Michigan Avenue
   - **C** McNichols Road
   - **D** Davison East

4. To go to the University of Detroit from her house near Warren West and Woodward Avenue, Julie would travel—
   - **A** north on Woodward Avenue, then west on McNichols Road
   - **B** north on Woodward Avenue, then east on Davison East
   - **C** west on Warren West, then north on Southfield Freeway
   - **D** east on Warren West, then south on Hwy. 75

5. Andy lives in Hamtramk. To get to River Rouge Park, he would travel generally—
   - **A** east
   - **B** west
   - **C** northeast
   - **D** southeast

Appendix

- **Answer Key**
- **Scoring Guidelines for Open-Ended Questions**
- **Scoring Rubrics for Open-Ended Questions**
- **Vocabulary List**
- **Answer Sheet**

Answer Key: Vocabulary

Practice 1 (p. 12)

1. C **2.** D **3.** C **4.** B **5.** D
6. C **7.** B **8.** A

Practice 2 (p. 13)

1. D **2.** B **3.** D **4.** C **5.** B
6. C **7.** B **8.** A

Practice 3 (p. 14)

1. D **2.** B **3.** C **4.** C **5.** D
6. B **7.** D **8.** A

Practice 4 (p. 15)

1. B **2.** D **3.** D **4.** B **5.** A
6. D **7.** B **8.** D

Practice 5 (p. 18)

1. B **2.** D **3.** C **4.** C **5.** C
6. A **7.** D **8.** C

Practice 6 (p. 17)

1. B **2.** D **3.** A **4.** C **5.** C
6. B **7.** A **8.** D

Practice 7 (p. 18)

1. C **2.** D **3.** A **4.** D **5.** B
6. C **7.** B **8.** C

Practice 8 (p. 19)

1. D **2.** B **3.** C **4.** C **5.** A
6. B **7.** D **8.** C

Practice 9 (p. 20)

1. C **2.** A **3.** D **4.** C **5.** C
6. B **7.** D **8.** B

Practice 10 (p. 21)

1. C **2.** A **3.** D **4.** D **5.** C
6. B **7.** C **8.** B

Practice 11 (p. 22)

1. B **2.** D **3.** D **4.** C **5.** C
6. D **7.** B **8.** A

Practice 12 (p. 23)

1. C **2.** B **3.** D **4.** D **5.** C
6. B **7.** C **8.** B

Practice 13 (p. 24)

1. D **2.** A **3.** C **4.** C **5.** D
6. B **7.** C **8.** D **9.** C **10.** D

Practice 14 (p. 25)

1. B **2.** D **3.** C **4.** C **5.** D
6. A **7.** D **8.** B **9.** C **10.** D

Practice 15 (p. 26)

1. D **2.** D **3.** C **4.** B **5.** A
6. B **7.** C **8.** D **9.** C **10.** C

Practice 16 (p. 27)

1. C **2.** A **3.** D **4.** C **5.** C
6. B **7.** D **8.** A **9.** C **10.** D

Practice 17 (p. 28)

1. C **2.** A **3.** D **4.** D **5.** B
6. C **7.** B **8.** D

Practice 18 (p. 29)

1. B **2.** C **3.** C **4.** C **5.** B
6. A **7.** D **8.** C

Practice 19 (p. 30)

1. D **2.** C **3.** B **4.** B **5.** C
6. A **7.** B **8.** C

Answer Key: Comprehension

1:Do you know how to study? (p. 32)

1. D **2.** A **3.** D **4.** C **5.** B
6. C **7.** B **8.** D **9.** B **10.** D
11. A **12.** C **13.** D **14.** B **15.** A
16. D **17. & 18.** See scoring guidelines and rubrics

2: It's a Bird's Life (p. 37)

1. B **2.** D **3.** C **4.** B **5.** D
6. C **7.** B **8.** C **9.** B **10.** B
11. A **12.** C **13.** B **14.** C **15.** C
16. & 17. See scoring guidelines and rubrics

3: Y-o-u-u Tom! (p. 43)

1. C **2.** A **3.** D **4.** C **5.** C
6. B **7.** D **8.** C **9.** D **10.** B
11. C **12.** D **13.** B **14.** A **15.** C
16. B **17., 18., & 19.** See scoring guidelines and rubrics

4: Cuckoos of the West (p. 50)

1. C **2.** C **3.** A **4.** C **5.** B
6. D **7.** C **8.** A **9.** B **10.** C
11. C **12.** D **13.** B **14.** C **15.** C
16. & 17. See scoring guidelines and rubrics

5: The Song of Hiawatha (p. 56)

1. D **2.** B **3.** C **4.** D **5.** A
6. B **7.** A **8.** C **9.** D **10.** B
11. C **12.** C **13.** A **14.** C **15.** D
16. & 17. See scoring guidelines and rubrics

6: A Race for Office (p. 61)

1. D **2.** C **3.** A **4.** D **5.** A
6. B **7.** C **8.** C **9.** C **10.** B
11. C **12.** B **13.** A **14.** D **15.** C
16. D **17.** See scoring guidelines and rubrics

7: The Girl in the Chicken Coop, Part I (p. 65)

1. D **2.** A **3.** C **4.** B **5.** A
6. D **7.** C **8.** C **9.** B **10.** D
11. D **12.** B **13.** D **14.** A **15.** B
16. C **17.** C **18.** A **19.** See scoring guidelines and rubrics

8: The Girl in the Chicken Coop, Part II (p. 70)

1. A **2.** C **3.** C **4.** B **5.** D
6. C **7.** B **8.** A **9.** C **10.** D
11. C **12.** D **13.** B **14.** C **15.** A
16. C **17.** A **18. & 19.** See scoring guidelines and rubrics

9: A Spring Event (p. 76)

1. B **2.** A **3.** D **4.** D **5.** C
6. B **7.** D **8.** C **9.** D **10.** B
11. A **12.** D **13.** B **14.** C **15.** B
16. D **17.** A
18. & 19. See scoring guidelines and rubrics

10: An Unfortunate Whale (p. 82)

1. B **2.** D **3.** D **4.** B **5.** A
6. D **7.** D **8.** C **9.** C **10.** A
11. B **12.** D **13.** B **14.** D **15.** C
16. & 17. See scoring guidelines and rubrics

11: What is El Niño? (p. 87)

1. B **2.** D **3.** D **4.** C **5.** D
6. B **7.** B **8.** C **9.** A **10.** C
11. A **12.** B **13.** See scoring guidelines and rubrics

10: The Indus Civilization (p. 91)

1. B **2.** D **3.** D **4.** A **5.** D
6. B **7.** C **8.** A **9.** D **10.** C
11. A **12.** C **13.** C **14.** B **15.** A
16. D **17.** A **18. & 19.** See scoring guidelines and rubrics

Answer Key: Study Skills

Practice 1 (p. 98)

1. D **2.** C **3.** D **4.** D

Practice 2 (p. 99)

1. C **2.** B **3.** C **4.** B **5.** B

Practice 3 (p. 100-101)

1. D **2.** B **3.** D **4.** C **5.** A
6. D **7.** C **8.** D

Practice 4 (p. 102-103)

1. C **2.** A **3.** C **4.** D **5.** B
6. D **7.** B **8.** C **9.** D **10.** C

Practice 5 (p. 104-105)

1. B **2.** D **3.** D **4.** C **5.** A
6. C **7.** C **8.** D **9.** C **10.** A

Practice 6 (p. 106)

1. C **2.** A **3.** D **4.** B **5.** D
6. C **7.** D

Practice 7 (p. 107)

1. D **2.** C **3.** C **4.** D **5.** B

Practice 8 (p. 108)

1. B **2.** D **3.** C **4.** C **5.** D **6.** B

Practice 9 (p. 109)

1. B **2.** D **3.** C **4.** C **5.** B
6. A **7.** C **8.** B **9.** C **10.** B

Practice 10 (p. 110)

1. D **2.** B **3.** C **4.** D **5.** B
6. D **7.** B **8.** D **9.** B **10.** D

Practice 11 (p. 111)

1. D **2.** A **3.** D **4.** C

Practice 12 (p. 112-113)

1. C **2.** D **3.** B **4.** D **5.** B
6. A **7.** C

Practice 13 (p. 114-115)

1. C **2.** D **3.** B **4.** D **5.** B
6. D **7.** B **8.** B **9.** C **10.** D

Practice 14 (p. 116)

1. C **2.** C **3.** D **4.** A **5.** B

Scoring Guidelines for Open-Ended Questions

Connect/Compare/Contrast

An effective response will include:

- a clear introduction that identifies the issues, characters, etc., to be connected, compared, and/or contrasted
- a clear, effective organizational plan to handle connections, similarities, and/or differences
- specific details that clearly identify connections, similarities, and/or differences
- clear transitions from one part of the response to another
- a clear, logical conclusion that summarizes the points made in the response

Use these scoring guidelines with the following open-ended questions—

"Cuckoos of the West," p. 54, #16*

**This question does not require a written composition as a response. To evaluate responses, focus on the student's selection/use of specific details and correct placement within the Venn diagram.*

Facts/Details

An effective response will include:

- facts that are pertinent to the main idea statement
- facts that are separate and distinct
- evidence of an understanding of the type of facts/details that logically support the given main idea
- evidence that a coherent paragraph could be written with the facts/details provided

Use these scoring guidelines with the following open-ended questions—

"An Unfortunate Whale," p. 85, #16*

**This question does not require a written composition as a response. To evaluate responses, focus on the student's selection and use of specific details that support the main idea statement.*

Follow Directions

An effective response will include:

- specific, delineated steps (in a process)
- consistent use of chronological order
- clear transitions from one step to the next
- specific details that clarify each step

Use these scoring guidelines with the following open-ended questions—

"A Spring Event," p. 81, #19*

**This question does not require a written composition as a response. To evaluate responses, focus on the student's selection and sequencing of the steps in a process.*

Genre Identification/Characteristics
Literary Elements/Figurative Language

When identifying the correct genre of a reading selection or the literary elements included in a selection, students should mention several of the following characteristics—

Fiction

- use of the basic elements (character, setting, problem, solution)
- sequence of events leading to a resolution (plot)
- purpose: to entertain

Nonfiction

- emphasis on factual events/information
- purpose: to explain, argue, persuade

Poetry

- use of stanza/verse form
- focus on sound devices (e.g., rhyme, alliteration, onomatopoeia)
- use of figurative language (e.g., similes, metaphors)

Use these scoring guidelines with the following open-ended questions—

"It's a Bird's Life," p. 42, #17
"Y-o-u-u Tom!" p. 47, #17
"Y-o-u-u Tom!" p. 48, #18
"The Song of Hiawatha," p. 59, #16
"The Song of Hiawatha," p. 60, #17*
"The Girl in the Chicken Coop, Part I," p. 69, #19

**This question does not require a written composition as a response. To evaluate responses, focus on the student's selection and use of specific details that support the conclusion/interpretation in the circle.*

Interpretations/Conclusions

An effective response will include:

- an introduction that clearly states the writer's opinion
- a clear, effective organizational plan
- appropriate and specific reasons that logically support the writer's position
- a clear, logical elaboration of reasons with facts, details, information, etc., from the text
- clear transitions from one part of the answer to another
- a clear, logical conclusion that summarizes the writer's position and reasons

Use these scoring guidelines with the following open-ended questions—

"It's a Bird's Life," p. 41, #16
"Cuckoos of the West," p. 55, #17*

**This question does not require a written composition as a response. To evaluate responses, focus on the student's selection and use of specific details that support the conclusion/interpretation in the circle.*

Paraphrase/Summarize

An effective response will include:

- a clear focus on the text's major ideas
- omission of extraneous details/information
- a clear, accurate statement of the text's basic message/content

Use these scoring guidelines with the following open-ended questions—

"The Girl in the Chicken Coop, Part II," p. 75, #19
"The Indus Civilization," p. 96, #19

Response to Text

An effective response will include:

- a clear focus on important ideas presented in the text
- a response that connects the text's major ideas to the writer's personal experiences and prior knowledge
- questions, speculations, or observations that relate logically and clearly to the text
- clear, logical elaboration of ideas with relevant information from both the text and the writer's experiences
- clear transitions from one part of the response to another
- a clear, logical conclusion that summarizes writer's response to the text

Use these scoring guidelines with the following open-ended questions—

"Do you know how to study?" p. 36, #18
"Y-o-u-u Tom!" p. 49, #19
"A Race for Office," p. 64, #17
"The Girl in the Chicken Coop, Part II," p. 74, #18
"A Spring Event," p. 80, #18
"An Unfortunate Whale," p. 86, #17
"The Indus Civilization," p. 95, #18

Text Structure

An effective response will include:

- information pertinent to the given passage
- obvious use of text structure to locate and organize information from the text
- evidence that a coherent paragraph or composition could be written with the information provided

Use these scoring guidelines with the following open-ended questions—

"Do you know how to study?" p. 35, #17*
"What is El Niño?" p. 90, #13*

**This question does not require a written composition as a response. To evaluate responses, focus on the student's selection and organization of information from the text.*

Scoring Rubrics for Open-Ended Questions

In most states that administer tests with open-ended questions requiring student-written responses, evaluators use scoring rubrics to assess these responses. A scoring rubric is an assessment tool designed to determine the degree to which a writer meets the established criteria for a given writing task.

Many scoring rubrics allow for holistic evaluation, which focuses on the overall effectiveness of the written response rather than individual errors in content, organization, mechanics, etc. For example, a scoring rubric might allow a teacher to score papers on a scale from 1 (for the least effective responses) to 4 (for the most effective responses). Rubrics that offer a broader scale of points (e.g., 1–6) allow for a more refined evaluation of a written response. For example, with these rubrics it is possible for evaluators to distinguish between an outstanding response (e.g., 6) and a very good response (e.g., 5). Rubrics with a narrow scale of points (e.g., 0–2) do not allow for a very refined evaluation, generally limiting evaluators to a response of either "pass" or "fail."

Sample scoring rubrics appear on the following pages. They offer several options for evaluating the written responses students complete for the open-ended questions in *TestSMART®*. A brief description of each rubric follows.

Note: Teachers may also use scoring rubrics provided for their own state's competency test.

Three-point rubric: This rubric has a narrow scale of points and, therefore, limits the scoring to basically pass–fail. The three-point rubric is most appropriate for brief written responses (2-4 sentences). In addition, this rubric works well with the short answers recorded on graphic organizers (e.g., Venn diagrams).

Four-point rubric: This rubric provides a wider scale of points, making a more refined evaluation possible. It does not, however, allow teachers to make clear distinctions between outstanding responses and those that are merely good. The four-point rubric is appropriate for brief written responses (2-4 sentences) and longer responses (two or more paragraphs).

Six-point rubric: Because of the broad scale of points, this rubric allows for a more refined evaluation of a written response. The six-point rubric is appropriate for longer responses (two or more paragraphs).

Three-Point Rubric

2	Provides complete, appropriate response Shows a thorough understanding Exhibits logical reasoning/conclusions Presents an accurate and complete response
1	Provides a partly inappropriate response Includes flawed reasoning/incorrect conclusions Overlooks part of question/task Presents an incomplete response Shows incomplete understanding
0	Indicates no understanding of reading selection Fails to respond to question/task

Four-Point Rubric

4	Focus on topic throughout response Thorough, complete ideas/information Clear organization throughout Logical reasoning/conclusions Thorough understanding of reading task Accurate, complete response
3	Focus on topic throughout most of response Many relevant ideas/pieces of information Clear organization throughout most of response Minor problems in logical reasoning/conclusions General understanding of reading task Generally accurate and complete response
2	Minimal focus on topic/task Minimally relevant ideas/information Obvious gaps in organization Obvious problems in logical reasoning/conclusions Minimal understanding of reading task Inaccuracies/incomplete response
1	Little or no focus on topic/task Irrelevant ideas/information No coherent organization Major problems in logical reasoning/conclusions Little or no understanding of reading task Generally inaccurate/incomplete response

Six-Point Rubric

6	Full focus on topic throughout response Thorough, complete ideas/information Clear, maintained organizational pattern throughout Clearly logical reasoning/conclusions Thorough understanding of reading task Accurate, complete response
5	Focus on topic throughout most of response Very thorough ideas/information Clear organization throughout majority of response Generally logical reasoning/conclusions Overall understanding of reading task Generally accurate and complete response
4	Focus on topic/task but with obvious minor digressions Sufficient relevant ideas/information Minor gaps in organization in parts of response Minor problems in logical reasoning/conclusions Above average understanding of reading task Minor inaccuracies that affect quality and thoroughness of response
3	Focus on topic/task but with obvious major digressions Relevant ideas/information mixed with irrelevant material Major gaps in organization Somewhat logical reasoning/conclusions Basic understanding of reading task Several inaccuracies that affect quality and thoroughness of response
2	Little or no focus on topic/task throughout response Few relevant ideas/pieces of information included in response Lack of organizational plan Illogical reasoning/conclusions throughout response Lack of basic understanding of reading task Generally inaccurate/incomplete response
1	Unacceptable response due to severe problems in focus, relevancy, organization, and/or logical reasoning/conclusions No understanding of reading task

Vocabulary List

absurd
abundant
accessory
acquaint
acquire
activate
acute
adhesive
administer
affectionate
agreeable
alliance
amend
amusement
annoy
antic
anxiety
apology
apparently
apply
approval
ardent
arid
artificial
assault
associate
association
astound
astronaut
astronomer
astronomy
atmosphere
authority
autobiography
banish
barrier
betray
biography
boulevard
brandish
brochure
brood
broth
brute
bulletin
cancel
capability
certainty
circumstance
clarify
clinch
coincidence
collision
competitor
complaint
complicate
complimentary
compound
comrade
conceal
condemn
confide
conscience
considerate
consideration
consist
constant
constrict
consult
consumer
contagious
controversy
convenient
cooperative
correspond
court
courtesy
covert
covet
credible
criticism
criticize
deceive
dedicate
dedication
defect
defense
defensive
demolish
departure
dependent
depress
depression
destination
destined
devastate
dialogue
disagreeable
discipline
disorder
display
dispute
distinct
distract
distrust
disturbance
drastic
dual
durable
dwell
dynamic
economic
economical
effective
eject
elated
elevate
enchantment
enforce
engrave
enlist
enthusiastic
entry
exact
exhilaration
exist
existence
expel
explosive
external
falsehood
fascinate
fascination
fashionable
fatal
feud
fidelity
filth
flaw
fluent
forerunner
foreseen
format
foundation
fracture
fringe
function
fundamental
gallery
garble
grieve
hasten
heed
hemisphere
heroic
hoist
honorable
ideal
idol
ignorance
illustrate
immerse
immigrant
immigrate
immovable
implement
implore
imprison
incredible
ingenious
ingratitude
install
institute
institution
insulate
intent
intention
interactive
interchange
interior

internal
irregular
jingle
jolt
jostle
judicial
keepsake
legible
lethal
limitation
malice
manhood
mar
mass
minimal
minimum
minor
misfit
mishandle
mishap
mobile
monopoly
mope
mutiny
navigate
navigation
navigator
neutral
nonresident
nonviolence
notify
observation
occupation
offspring
pamphlet
paralyze
parson
particle
patriotic
pension
perceive
perceptive
percussion
persecute
perspire
persuasive
phenomenon
plague
political
possess
potential
predictable
preface
preference
prejudice
previous
privacy
probability
profitable
proposal
provoke
publicity
purity
pursuit
qualification
qualify
query
radiant
recital
recitation
recite
recollect
recycle
refusal
regardless
reliable
repetition
resemble
resident
resistance
restless
restlessness
restrict
revolt
rind
rural
sanitary
satisfactory
savor
scanty
scenic
seasonal
semicircle
semifinal
sentimental
session
shroud
similarity
simplicity
simulate
sleek
slogan
spectacular
spiritual
splendor
sponsor
standardize
stature
stingy
strangle
strenuous
succession
sufficient
suitable
supervisor
suspend
sympathetic
sympathize
sympathy
tactic
temperament
tension
thorough
thrive
tolerable
tonic
tragic
treacherous
trespass
tyranny
unqualified
unreliable
urgent
vaccinate
variation
veer
verbal
vicinity
victorious
violate
vista
visual
vital
vivid
voluntary
wedge
wilt
wit
worthy
wrath

Name ______________________________ **Date** ____________

Comprehension: Passage # _______ **Vocabulary:** Practice # _______

Study Skills: Practice # _______

Answer Sheet

1.	Ⓐ	Ⓑ	Ⓒ	Ⓓ	**10.**	Ⓐ	Ⓑ	Ⓒ	Ⓓ
2.	Ⓐ	Ⓑ	Ⓒ	Ⓓ	**11.**	Ⓐ	Ⓑ	Ⓒ	Ⓓ
3.	Ⓐ	Ⓑ	Ⓒ	Ⓓ	**12.**	Ⓐ	Ⓑ	Ⓒ	Ⓓ
4.	Ⓐ	Ⓑ	Ⓒ	Ⓓ	**13.**	Ⓐ	Ⓑ	Ⓒ	Ⓓ
5.	Ⓐ	Ⓑ	Ⓒ	Ⓓ	**14.**	Ⓐ	Ⓑ	Ⓒ	Ⓓ
6.	Ⓐ	Ⓑ	Ⓒ	Ⓓ	**15.**	Ⓐ	Ⓑ	Ⓒ	Ⓓ
7.	Ⓐ	Ⓑ	Ⓒ	Ⓓ	**16.**	Ⓐ	Ⓑ	Ⓒ	Ⓓ
8.	Ⓐ	Ⓑ	Ⓒ	Ⓓ	**17.**	Ⓐ	Ⓑ	Ⓒ	Ⓓ
9.	Ⓐ	Ⓑ	Ⓒ	Ⓓ	**18.**	Ⓐ	Ⓑ	Ⓒ	Ⓓ